Praise for

Becoming a Vessel of God's Power

"Partow's voice shines through her own and others' stories, as she sprinkles her anecdotes with doses of humor and forthrightness.... Partow's love for God and women is evident throughout. Women looking for hope and a good kick in the pants will find it here."

—*Publishers Weekly*

"Donna Partow is a stick of dynamite for the soul sick and tired of being stuck in the mundane. For every woman who has ever wanted to do something significant for God...Donna not only challenges women to rise up and take their place in the kingdom, she encourages them to allow the Lord to take their ordinary lives and make something extraordinary out of everything they do."

—JOANNA WEAVER, best-selling author of *Having a Mary Heart in a Martha World*

"Like healing salve on a wounded heart.... We all long to make a difference for God. Donna Partow combines vulnerability and boldness, with the strong foundation of scriptural truth, to help us on the journey of finding our purpose."

—ALLISON GAPPA BOTTKE, speaker and author of *God Allows U-Turns* and debut novel *A Stitch in Time*

"If you want to shine for Jesus...Donna Partow writes a roadmap of the life every Christian should aspire to live. Convicting and convincing.... Superb wisdom and communication shine through."

—WAYNE ATCHESON, Christian Writers Guild

"Donna has something to say to everyone: the new Christian, the seasoned believer, and the still-searching."

  —NANCY KARPENSKE, contributing editor of *Christian*
   Standard magazine and director of women's ministry at
   LifeBridge Christian Church in Longmont, Colorado

"She writes with appealing vulnerability...successfully conveys a message of hope to readers who are disillusioned with their lives."

  —Crosswalk.com

"Donna Partow is refreshingly, gut-wrenchingly honest. She minces no words, cuts straight through the masks, and opens her soul. A rare Christian book."

  —BECKY FREEMAN, author of *Worms in My Tea and Other*
   Mixed Blessings

"Most of us ache to be more like Jesus.... Donna walks us through this process. It isn't easy. It costs us dearly. But it changes our lives completely."

  —SHEILA WALSH, author of *Honestly*

"If you're stuck in a rut in your personal Bible study...or you long for God to use you in fresh ways...or you and your small group are tired of pat answers...this book is for you!"

  —SUSAN YATES, author of *A House Full of Friends*

"Donna imparts new meaning to the themes of repentance, redemption, and revival. Her brave honesty invites the hurting and hassled heart to drink deeply at the well-spring of Christ's irresistible grace."

  —DEBRA EVANS, author of *Women of Character*

Becoming
a Vessel of
God's Power

BECOMING
A VESSEL OF
GOD'S POWER

Give God Thirty Days and See What He Will Do

DONNA PARTOW

WATERBROOK
PRESS

BECOMING A VESSEL OF GOD'S POWER
PUBLISHED BY WATERBROOK PRESS
12265 Oracle Boulevard, Suite 200
Colorado Springs, Colorado 80921
A division of Random House Inc.

Details in some anecdotes and stories have been changed to protect the identities of the persons involved.

ISBN 978-1-57856-960-1

Published in association with the literary agency of Alive Communications Inc., 7680 Goddard Street, Suite 200, Colorado Springs, CO 80920, www.alivecommunications.com.

Library of Congress Cataloging-in-Publication Data
Partow, Donna.
    Becoming a vessel of God's power : give God thirty days and see what he will do / Donna Partow.
— 1st ed.
        p. cm.
Includes bibliographical references.
ISBN 978-1-57856-960-1
        1. Christian women—Religious life. 2. Spiritual life—Christianity. 3. Christian life. I. Title.
BV4527.P3725 2007
248.8'43—dc22

                                                                2007005122

Printed in the United States of America
2007—First Edition

10 9 8 7 6 5 4 3 2 1

This book is for my daughters, who daily demonstrate power-packed faith:

Leah, thank you for being my "hypocrisy litmus tester." You continually challenge me and give me incentive to resist the ever-present temptation to write one thing while living another. Thanks for keepin' it real. You are a mighty woman of God.

Tara, your unconditional love and genuine compassion for others is such an inspiration. You are the hands and feet of Jesus. I need to become more like you.

CONTENTS

Sing to God, O kingdoms of the earth,
  sing praise to the Lord,
  Selah
to him who rides the ancient skies above,
  who thunders with mighty voice.
Proclaim the power of God,
  whose majesty is over Israel,
  whose power is in the skies.
You are awesome, O God, in your sanctuary;
  the God of Israel gives power and strength
    to his people.
Praise be to God!

PSALM 68:32–35

Experience the Real Thing

The kingdom of God is not a matter
of talk but of power.
1 Corinthians 4:20

A freight train full of roaring lions.

At a distance but closing in fast.

That's what it sounded like. Then the floor beneath me started shaking. The room began swaying from side to side. As I stood on the eighteenth floor of the Ala Moana Hotel on Oahu, my first thought was that I was imagining things. It occurred to me that I might be physically ill and about to pass out. But as my ten-year-old daughter sat up in the bed, looking equally alarmed, I realized we were in the midst of an earthquake. Six point seven on the Richter scale, I later learned—the largest to hit the Hawaiian Islands in more than fifty years.

Miraculously, God enabled me to remain uncharacteristically calm. Tara and I quickly dressed and headed out into the hallway. Before we made it to the stairwell, all the lights went out and we were engulfed in darkness. Feeling our way down the stairs, we soon encountered a growing throng of frightened hotel guests. I missed a step, twisting my ankle, but we pressed onward, inching our way through the dark, finally making it down to the street below. Just when we didn't think matters could get any worse, we stepped outside into pouring rain.

I struck up a crisis-driven friendship with a doctor and her husband who agreed to let us hop in their car, and we drove away from the towering buildings. We wanted to be as far from concrete and glass as we could possibly get if any strong aftershocks hit. After about thirty minutes, I looked at my watch and announced, "I'm scheduled to speak at the hotel in five minutes!" We decided the worst was behind us, and the couple agreed to drive me back to the Ala Moana where, sure enough, many of the retreat attendees were standing outside, wondering what to do.

I had previously been in several conferences that had been disrupted by fire alarms, but in every case, it turned out to be a false alarm. That was distressing enough. This was the real thing. A real-life disaster. Calling it an act of nature or an act of God, people were reminded once again that life doesn't always turn out the way we plan. We had all been shaken with a fresh realization that there are forces at work more powerful than any human being.

I think that's a good thing. It's so easy to deceive ourselves into thinking we've got the world figured out and under control. But in life, as in earthquake-prone regions, every once in a while, God lets everything that can shake, shake. Whatever is left standing is a foundation worth building on.

The hotel staff set votive candles along the floor, creating a path through the lobby and up the stalled escalators, guiding the way to our second-floor conference room. Here, a continental breakfast awaited those of us attending the Salvation Army Pacific Region women's retreat. The candles also lit the way for everyone else who was frightened, hungry, and desperate for that first cup of coffee. People began streaming in. Pandemonium doesn't begin to describe it. Unfazed, the conference director,

Major Jonette Mulch, simply smiled and said, "We're the Salvation Army. This is what we do. We feed people." Then she started singing. And she kept on singing. And the women sang. And they kept on singing.

We sang "This Little Light of Mine" and "He's Got the Whole World in His Hands." We sang "Shout to the Lord" and dozens of old praise choruses. I delivered a short message on what it means for Christians to be a light in the darkness. Ironically, that was my planned message, even though I hadn't planned to deliver it by candlelight! A woman pulled out her ukulele, and we sang some more. A hotel guest walked up and started drumming along, then shared how much our impromptu church service meant to him. Other guests expressed the same sentiment.

We welcomed everyone who entered, offering them breakfast and a word of encouragement. We laughed, we cried, we prayed, we hugged, and we sang. My daughter went around the room, hugging people who looked as if they needed hugs. Later she passed out handmade bookmarks that she had made by candlelight. She even did cartwheels in order to entertain some small children whose parents had come into the room, wondering what all the singing and laughing was about.

A group of Polynesian women from a homeless shelter on Maui performed a hula dance as they sang praise to God. Micronesian women from the Marshall Islands, many of whom never have electricity anyway, worshiped God in their own language and with their own form of dance. An African American woman belted out "Amazing Grace" as if she meant it with all her heart. And she did. We all did. We knew we served an amazing God and that we were part of something amazing. We had witnessed God's power. We knew it. Everyone in the room knew it, even those who did not yet know God personally.

We had experienced the power of God. Not in the earthquake, but in its aftermath. Not in what shook, but in what had not been shaken: our faith, our hope, and our love. Those three things remained. Later that day, many of these same women found themselves stranded at the airport. Rather than wallowing in self-pity, they continued singing and helped serve more than three thousand free meals (compliments of the Salvation Army) to fellow travelers.

The electrical power in the hotel remained off all day, giving me ample time to ponder the power of God—the power I had seen demonstrated *after* the earthquake. I couldn't help thinking about Elijah. Shortly after seeing God send fire from heaven in response to his prayers, Elijah was so discouraged that he hid out in a cave. God came and gave him these instructions: "Go out and stand on the mountain in the presence of the LORD, for the LORD is about to pass by" (1 Kings 19:11). No doubt Elijah expected to witness the power of God in yet another dramatic fashion. But that's not what happened. "Then a great and powerful wind tore the mountains apart and shattered the rocks before the LORD, but the LORD was not in the wind. After the wind there was an earthquake, but the LORD was not in the earthquake. After the earthquake came a fire, but the LORD was not in the fire. And after the fire came a gentle whisper" (1 Kings 19:11–12).

Finally, I understood. God's power isn't always where we expect to find it.

For many months leading up to the earthquake, I had been thinking, praying, and attempting to write about the power of God. It seemed to be the missing ingredient in the lives of many Christians. Unfortunately, I spent much of my so-called writing time staring at my blank computer screen. Hours turned into days and days turned into months as I sat with motionless fingers, wondering if I was the only one agonizing over the lack of power in the lives of so many Christians. The blank computer screen stared back at me, defying me to write something worth reading. A contemptuous voice kept whispering in my ear, *This is a stupid waste of time; you're just obsessed with something no one else cares about.*

The blank screen prevailed until one Sunday morning. Waiting for the worship service to begin, I thumbed casually through the church bulletin. The day's sermon topic? You guessed it: the power of God. My pastor preached with tremendous passion and urgency. Every word he spoke confirmed everything God had been showing me about the need for Christ's followers to begin walking in the power of God. At the end of the service, my pastor did something I've never seen him do. Before asking for new believers to come forward, he invited anyone who wanted to experience more of God's power to come to the altar. Hundreds, including me, poured forward, tears streaming, hands lifted, hearts crying out to God in desperation. It was a dramatic display of emotion rarely seen at our fairly subdued, suburban megachurch. By taking the socially risky step of getting up out of their pews, they made a bold statement for all to see: *I want to experience the power of God, and I don't care who knows it. What I have is not enough, and I'm willing to admit it.* In that moment, I knew I wasn't alone. I believe millions of Christians are yearning to experience the power of God. We want to taste it, not just read about it in the Bible or church-history books, not just hear what's taking place in Uganda or China. We want to see God's power in our own lives, in our families, in our churches, and in our nation.

We want a clear, dramatic, immediate, unmistakable, life-altering encounter with the transforming power of God. Throughout the Bible, when God showed up, everyone knew it. Joseph went from a prison to a palace overnight. Peter led three thousand to Christ with one sermon. The walls of Jericho fell with a shout. The waters of the Jordan parted while the Israelites slept. When that fire fell from heaven on Elijah's sacrifice, it didn't start as a spark to get a fire going. It fell in a consuming fire, demonstrating the overwhelming power of God. But God also demonstrated his power when he cared enough to track Elijah down and speak to him in a whisper. Sometimes God's power is revealed in powerful circumstances;

sometimes it manifests in powerful demonstrations of his personal care for his children.

The world needs to see both, just as the hotel guests did when they wandered into our postearthquake worship service. Today, people around the world look at Christians in frustration and say, "Show us the power! If your God is real, if your faith is true, why isn't it working?" Good question. Wimpy excuses just won't do anymore. Our lives need to be distinctively different. Not only do our actions need to be different, but so do our reactions to the earthquakes of life. We need to leave people scratching their heads in wonder. Like Shadrach, Meshach, and Abednego, our faith needs to be so power packed that it enables us to boldly say, "We'd rather make fools of ourselves expecting God to do something dramatic and lifesaving than meander through life, claiming to believe something we don't really believe. In fact, we're so sure of God's power, we're willing to stake our lives on it." Shadrach, Meshach, and Abednego walked straight into a fiery furnace. God didn't snuff out the flames; instead, he walked through the fire with them and enabled them to come through unscathed and unbowed (see Daniel 3).

God did not spare Christians from experiencing the earthquake in Hawaii. He didn't demonstrate his power by holding our hotel steady while the rest of the island shook. Instead, he held us and enabled us to smile and sing—he granted us the power to shake without being shaken.

Do you long to experience the power of God—and not just experience it for yourself, but to demonstrate it to a watching world? Is it the cry of your heart as well? If so, you've picked up the right book.

One lesson God has determinedly taught me, over and over again, is this: the world doesn't need to see what we can do for God; the world needs to see something only God can do. Only the power of God can transform a heart, a family, a city, or a nation. Only the power of God can bring about lasting change in people and circumstances. We cannot manufacture the power of God. Yes, we can create religious programs and activities, but they'll never take the place of the power of God. And because programs lack true power, the minute they end, their impact on people's lives declines. That's why too many churches have become Activity Generating Stations rather than conduits for God's power, and that's why so many Christians are trapped on the treadmill of church busyness rather than living the Great Adventure that God has ordained for us.

When I knelt down, alone beside a quiet riverbank, and surrendered my life to God in 1980, my heart longed for two things: to be different and to make a difference in the world. I believed God could transform my life and use me to help transform the world—well, at least a small corner of it. Although I've taken many missteps and endured some painful misadventures along the way, those two dreams have remained foremost in my mind. As a result, I've spent more than twenty-five years studying the power of God, determined to discover how God radically transforms a person and how one individual can touch the world in a significant way. This book is the fruit of that ongoing quest.

I want to help you understand what we can do to allow God to change us into conduits for his power. In *Becoming a Vessel of God's Power* you'll discover:

- *Power through purification.* God's power flows most consistently through a pure vessel, so you'll learn some practical ways you can experience ongoing spiritual purity.
- *The power of the Word.* You'll see how to tap into the power of God's Word with a fresh approach to reading, memorization, meditation, and usage.
- *The power of prayer.* You'll find some practical tools for unlocking the power of praying Scripture for yourself, plus the effectiveness

of God-directed prayer, corporate prayer, and praying with
authority.

- *God's provision for power.* You'll learn to make the most of what
  God has provided for you to walk in his power, including the
  support of prayer warriors, insightful counselors, and gifted
  teachers.

- *The power of balancing solitude and service.* You'll be challenged to
  balance rest and service, in order to strengthen both the internal
  reality of God's Spirit at work within you and the external expression of the Holy Spirit's power upon you, enabling you to impact
  people and situations.

- *Power in practice.* You'll discover that as you walk in obedience
  and listen to God's Spirit, he directs you to situations where his
  power is already at work. You simply get the joy of being part
  of it.

If that sounds like what you're looking for, I challenge you to make a
serious commitment. Right now. Make the decision. For the next thirty
days, open your mind, your heart, and your life to the power of God. Give
God thirty days—and see what he will do! Each day along your journey
to becoming a vessel of God's power includes a Scripture verse to meditate on, a prayer to pray aloud, a truth to affirm, five questions for reflection, an action assignment, and an opportunity for you to write out your
own prayer to God. (If you would like to do this study with a group,
there's a free Leader's Guide available at www.donnapartow.com/power.)

I pray that before you've finished this book, you will see a powerful
move of God in and through your life. That's a bold prayer, but we have
a bold God and a bold book (the Bible) filled with bold promises. Don't
settle for cheap substitutes; God wants you to experience his power in you
and through you. Are you ready to experience the real thing? If so, let's go!

Dear heavenly Father, I want to experience your power. I want to know, not just believe, that you are awesome in power and mighty in deeds! I'm willing to openly admit that I need more of you in my life. I invite you, Holy Spirit, to be my Teacher and Coach for these thirty days. My heart is open to whatever you want to do in and through my life. Amen.

AFFIRM

I can experience the power of God.

APPLY

1. When you think of the power of God, what's the first biblical example that comes to mind?

   _____

   _____

   _____

2. Do you believe God can still demonstrate his power in similar ways? Why or why not?

_____

_____

_____

3. What is the most dramatic example of the power of God you know of? (Perhaps someone you know was miraculously healed, or you heard about a miracle from a missionary, and so on.)

_____

_____

_____

4. How have you witnessed the power of God at work in your own life?

_____

_____

_____

5. What are your hopes for this thirty-day journey?

_____

_____

_____

ℐCT

1. Purchase a spiral-bound notebook of 3 x 5 inch white or multi-colored index cards (widely available wherever office supplies are sold). If you'd like, decorate and even laminate the cover.

   Each day, record the daily Affirm statement (for example: "I can experience the power of God") along with the day's Scripture verse. Use the reverse side to record key points from this book and other sources, such as songs, sermons, radio programs, and poems.

   As you ask the Holy Spirit to teach you about the power of God, he will answer that prayer with insights that go well beyond this book. Record those insights in your index-card notebook. Carry it with you wherever you go. Jot down thoughts, Scripture, and God-ordained experiences.

   I have dozens of such index-card notebooks, and each one is a special treasure, reminding me of the power of God operating in my own life.

2. Write out today's affirmation and scripture on the first index card.

3. Write out your own prayer, expressing what God has shown you today about his mighty power.

Believe God Is Still a God of Power

You are the God who performs miracles;
you display your power among the peoples.

PSALM 77:14

*T*he year was 1979. James and Cynthia were collecting welfare and living in a housing project in Nashville, Tennessee. Although unmarried, they had five children, including a son James had fathered during a previous marriage. Once upon a time, both James and Cynthia had heard the claims of Christ and mentally assented to the truth of the gospel. But they weren't walking with God, which meant they were a long way from experiencing power-packed faith.

All that was about to change.

When Cynthia went to the doctor for her six-week checkup after the birth of their fifth child, she learned she was pregnant, *again.* The couple couldn't afford another mouth to feed, so they quickly found a place that offered free abortions. On the morning of the scheduled abortion, James and Cynthia discovered that the batteries had been stolen from *both* of their vehicles, even though their cars were parked on opposite sides of a huge parking lot. Strangely enough, no other batteries in the area had been stolen that night.

James borrowed money from a relative and replaced the batteries, while Cynthia rescheduled the abortion for the following week. However, after they woke up on the appointed day, they again discovered that their vehicles had been deliberately targeted. This time all four tires on *both* cars were flattened. Amazingly enough, they still didn't take the hint! All they could think about was the impossibility of their financial situation and that the only solution was for Cynthia to have an abortion. So they rescheduled again and contacted a relative who agreed to drive them to the clinic.

Cynthia went through the paperwork and was taken into a back room. As she sat waiting for the doctor, she heard a commanding voice say, *Get off the table.* She got up, shaken to the depths of her being, and rushed out of the building. She had heard the voice of God—and she knew it. Suddenly, she realized that God had been trying to block the abortion all along. When she and James refused to listen to what God was saying to them through their circumstances, God powerfully intervened just moments before it would have been too late.

God had Cynthia's undivided attention. He had more in store for her husband.

Cynthia gave birth to a son on April 28, 1980. It "just so happened" to be the same date that James's oldest son had been born six years earlier, the son from whom James was estranged. God spoke to James, warning him, *If you don't make drastic changes in your life and begin to follow me, you will lose all your children just as you feel you've lost your oldest son.*

The couple got involved in a local church and were married in October of that same year. In time, James became an elder in their church. In June 1995, he became an ordained minister and now serves as the senior pastor at Bride of Christ Church in Nashville.

In case you have been wondering if God still intervenes in the world today, I trust this story puts your doubts to rest. God is still a God of power; he still forcefully advances his purposes in this world and in our lives. Lest you think this tale is fresh from Internet Urban Legendville, let me tell you how I know it is true. The child rescued from that abortion helps lead worship at my home church, a five-thousand-member congregation in Mesa, Arizona. Nick Oldham is truly a gift from God whose tremendous voice, contagious smile, and passion for God are a blessing to every life he touches.

Nick's parents told him about the near abortion when he was thirteen years old. He had always had a profound sense of purpose and demonstrated leadership ability from a young age, but when he heard how God had intervened to save his life, he felt overwhelmed with the love of God. Since then, he has devoted himself to studying God's Word—and it shows. Nick is a living, breathing miracle.

Throughout Scripture, God's power is often (although not always) equated with miraculous events: the creation of the world, the plagues upon Egypt, the parting of the Red Sea, the floating of the ax head, the ushering of Elijah into heaven in a whirlwind, the defeat of Sennacherib's vast army, the impregnation of Mary, the works and resurrection of Jesus. I've heard many people wonder aloud if God still works miracles today. Some Christians believe that miracles ended with the New Testament era. Many have asked me why I believe otherwise. That's an important question that can't be answered in a day, but we shall make a beginning.

God has demonstrated his mighty power in and through the lives of his people in every century since the Holy Spirit descended on the Day of Pentecost. I've listened to countless people around the world testify that they have personally experienced the power of God. Although some

Christians greet all such reports with skepticism, we are supposed to be *believers,* not doubters.

Of course, people doubted Jesus when he walked the earth, performing miracles before their very eyes. We should not be surprised when people today have doubts. Nevertheless, Jesus rebuked the Pharisees for their doubt: "You are in error because you do not know the Scriptures or the power of God" (Matthew 22:29). These men devoted themselves to studying the Old Testament, yet Jesus said they were *in error* because they didn't truly *know* God's Word. They knew about the Bible, but theirs was a dry, dead religion because they lacked the power of God.

Are sincere Christians today sometimes guilty of knowing about God without experiencing his power? Do some of us have powerless faith, rather than power-packed faith? I believe the answer is yes. The good news is: God's power *is* available. Since you've read this far, I know you believe that. Rest assured that God will honor you for seeking more of him, just as he has honored others throughout the ages. God made it a priority to point out that he is the same from generation to generation: "I change not" (Malachi 3:6, KJV). Whatever God has done in generations past, he can do today. If you question whether Christians can still experience the power of God, please open your heart as you meditate on the following passages:

"Jesus Christ is the same yesterday and today and forever" (Hebrews 13:8). If Jesus lives in us, and he is still the same as he was when he walked the earth, then he is still in the miracle-working business. The only difference is that now he desires to work miracles *through us.*

"Since the creation of the world God's invisible qualities—his eternal power and divine nature—have been clearly seen, being understood from what has been made, so that men are without excuse" (Romans 1:20). God's power is *eternal.* That means he can re-create us—with the same power he unleashed to create the earth—into people who unleash the kingdom of God upon the earth. He can clearly and convincingly answer our prayers when we ask that his kingdom come and his will be done, here on earth as it is in heaven.

"O LORD, God of our fathers, are you not the God who is in heaven? You rule over all the kingdoms of the nations. Power and might are in your hand, and no one can withstand you" (2 Chronicles 20:6). No one has snatched power and might away from God! He still holds power in his hands, and he still extends his hands to and through us.

"You are awesome, O God, in your sanctuary; the God of Israel gives power and strength to his people" (Psalm 68:35). We still serve a God who gives power and strength to his people. In addition to the oft-uttered prayer, *God, give me strength,* we can also pray, *God, give me power. Make me a vessel of your power.*

"Praise be to the name of God for ever and ever; wisdom and power are his" (Daniel 2:20). Daniel goes on to write: "I thank and praise you, O God of my fathers: You have given me wisdom and power" (verse 23). The same God who imparted those attributes to Daniel will make them available to us today. Just as Christians don't hesitate to ask God for wisdom, we can ask for power, expecting God to answer affirmatively.

"But we have this treasure in jars of clay to show that this all-surpassing power is from God and not from us" (2 Corinthians 4:7). Christians proclaim all the time, "I'm not perfect; I'm just a jar of clay." We acknowledge that the first half of the verse applies to contemporary believers. Well, the second half applies as well. The reason God created us as "jars of clay" was not to help us make excuses for bad behavior, but *so we could display the power of God.* The Bible not only says we can display the power of God, it commands us to do so: "Finally, be strong in the Lord and in his mighty power" (Ephesians 6:10).

As we study the Bible and church history, we must conclude that God was, is, and always will be a God who displays his power. Quite frankly,

God is a bit of a show-off! He loves to make "a public spectacle" of "the powers and authorities," as he did on the cross (Colossians 2:15).

God is, always has been, and always will be, a God of power. God always has and always will demonstrate his power in and through his people. He can and will enable *you* to experience that power. No doubt about it.

Dear heavenly Father, thank you for making your intentions plain. From the beginning of time, from the moment of creation, you have shown your power. Throughout Scripture, you've demonstrated that power through frail human beings. Forgive me for ignoring your command to be strong in your mighty power. Help me to open my eyes to the truth of your Word and open my heart to experiencing your power. I'm so thankful that you are a God who performs miracles, a God who delights in displaying power. Make me your vessel. Amen.

AFFIRM

I remain confident that God is still a God of power.

APPLY

1. Describe a time when you needed wisdom and God supplied it.

   _____

   _____

   _____

2. Describe a time or situation when you needed God's special strength and he imparted it to you.

   _____

   _____

   _____

3. If God still imparts wisdom and strength to his people, why would he stop imparting power? If he does impart power, should we pray for it? Why or why not?

   _____

   _____

   _____

4. Can you list other scriptures that give evidence that God still exercises power today? Or, can you give contemporary examples of God's power at work?

   _____

   _____

   _____

5. Describe the most powerful spiritual experience you've ever had.

_____

_____

_____

*A*CT

1. List several areas where you need to experience the power of God in your life right now. Commit to pray over these daily.
2. Write out today's affirmation and scripture in your index-card notebook.
3. Write out your own prayer, expressing what God has shown you today about his mighty power.

_____

_____

_____

_____

Remember What God Has Done

I will remember the deeds of the LORD;
yes, I will remember your miracles of long ago.
I will meditate on all your works
and consider all your mighty deeds.

PSALM 77:11–12

I just witnessed the power of God in a parking lot. I have been listening to stories of power-packed faith all weekend long while eavesdropping on casual conversations among a group of men on their annual guys-only retreat.[1] Some recalled how God had transformed their marriages; others remembered how they came to know Jesus in the first place. Some recounted tales of instant deliverance from drugs and alcohol, while others encouraged a young man to "keep believing" for his deliverance.

But what touched me most was the living testimony I saw with my own eyes. Men from every conceivable background, walking shoulder to shoulder, exchanging bear hugs and robust pats on the back. Young men covered in tattoos, old men crowned with gray hair. Native Americans,

African Americans, Hispanics, Caucasians—I think every tribe and tongue was represented. As they bid their farewells to one another, I stood on the edge of the parking lot and cried. These men had such genuine love for God and one another that if I could have bottled it, I would've become an overnight millionaire.

The world needs to see and hear much more of such testimonies from the church. It needs to encounter living examples of what the power of God can do and what he has already done. One of the most unfortunate trends in churches today is that one person often does all the speaking. Gone are the days of the old congregational church when *anyone* and *everyone* in the congregation could (and often would!) stand to share a testimony of what God had done in his or her life.

One of the greatest gifts God has given—and one of the most powerful tools for strengthening our faith—is the testimony of the saints, past and present. In this rationalistic age we tend to minimize the significance of personal testimony. We want incontrovertible, scientific fact. We want DNA evidence. But the truth remains: God says human testimony is a powerful force. "They overcame him by the blood of the Lamb and by the word of their testimony" (Revelation 12:11). If the word of our testimony is enough to overcome the Evil One, imagine its power in the lives of people we encounter. As I often say, people can argue with your politics, they can argue with your theology, but no one can argue with your testimony. Your story of God's faithfulness, backed up by a life lived out of gratitude for what he has done, is a powerful weapon of spiritual warfare.

Every Christian has a testimony of God's power. Mine is that God instantly delivered me from drug addiction. Yours may be that God loved you enough to place you in a wonderful Christian home, with parents who taught you the truth of God's Word from an early age. Your testimony may be that God saved you from the mess you had made of your life or that your family has walked with God for countless generations. Whatever it is, your story is your story. No one can take it from you. But they do need to hear it from you!

Of course, some people respond to testimonies of God's power with skepticism, "We're just trying to be levelheaded. Those claims fly in the face of scientific evidence, so they couldn't possibly be true." Well, the last time I checked, that's precisely what a *miracle* is. Something that flies in the face of scientific evidence and couldn't possibly happen apart from supernatural intervention. Did Jesus say, "When I return, will I find levelheadedness on the earth?" No, he said, "Will I find faith?" (see Luke 18:8).

Honestly, levelheadedness doesn't impress God. Faith impresses God. So don't worry about the skeptics. Continue to give your testimony, confident that some *will* believe that what God has done for you, he can do for them. Take time, even now, to reflect upon the story of God's working in your life and the story of his work throughout your family's history. I would encourage you not only to reflect but to *write it down*. Record it so that future generations will be blessed. Write down examples of God's faithfulness *daily* in a spiritual journal. When my friend Susan's mother died, the family uncovered a mountain of spiritual journals (including prayers, sermon notes, and quotes from Christian books) and a well-worn Bible filled with margin notes of what God was teaching her, how she was praying, and the promises she was clinging to. What a rich, spiritual treasury she left behind for her family! It makes me ask, *When I'm gone, what will my children uncover? Am I leaving behind a record of God's blessing—or just a litany of my own complaints? Uh-oh!*

We humans are a forgetful people. We focus on what we need right now, forgetting how God has met our needs in the past. That's why he commands us, over and over, to remember. The word *remember* occurs 162 times in the Bible, including:

- "Remember well what the LORD your God did" (Deuteronomy 7:18).
- "Remember how the LORD your God led you all the way" (8:2).
- "Remember that you were slaves" (16:12).
- "I will remember the deeds of the LORD; yes, I will remember your miracles of long ago. I will meditate on all your works and consider all your mighty deeds" (Psalm 77:11–12).

If we want to become vessels of God's power, we need to make a conscious decision: I *will* remember. I *will* remember the deeds and the miracles God has performed, yes, even those performed long ago. Remembering what God has done is a choice. He doesn't want us to remember for remembering's sake, but so we'll have the faith to believe that what he *has done before,* he can *do right now.*

Ask your parents (or other mature Christians) to recall stories of God's intervention, and then tell these to your children. And don't just tell these stories once, but tell them over and over again. I live in a neighborhood that is 80 percent Mormon. I can't help but admire their commitment to preserving family history. One neighbor, Beth, is always telling me tales of how her ancestors set out from the East Coast with all their possessions in a wheelbarrow, heading for the promised land of Salt Lake City. Shouldn't we be telling *our* children stories of *our* faith?

Our faith begins with the faith of our fathers, from Abraham to the apostles. God preserved his Word for our sake: "For everything that was written in the past was written to teach us, so that through endurance and the encouragement of the Scriptures we might have hope" (Romans 15:4). That's why it's so important to study the Bible and read the testimonies of God's people. We cannot remember something we don't take time to learn in the first place.

Shortly after Moses died, Joshua assumed command and led the people of Israel across the miraculously parted Jordan River and on to the

Promised Land. But before they rushed off to settle into homes they hadn't built to work in fields they hadn't planted, God told them to stop and set up stones of remembrance. Joshua appointed twelve men, instructing each to select a large stone from the middle of the Jordan riverbed. These would serve as constant reminders of the miracle God had performed. They were also a great conversation starter: "In the future, when your children ask you, 'What do these stones mean?' tell them that the flow of the Jordan was cut off before the ark of the covenant of the LORD. When it crossed the Jordan, the waters of the Jordan were cut off. These stones are to be a memorial to the people of Israel forever" (Joshua 4:6–7).

God wants us to remember who he is, what he's done, and what he's capable of doing. That way when we face obstacles, as we surely will, our hearts won't faint. Our stones of remembrance will also be a witness to our children that our faith is *real*. Why not set up your own stones of remembrance? Remember all that God has done for you: the times he has spoken clearly, the prayers he has answered, the miracles he has performed. I know it's hard to remember the details, but that's *exactly why* it's so important to write them down. Once you've written your list, copy it into the front of your Bible and keep it up to date as God continues to work miracles in your life.

In the front of my Bible I've written:

- Fifth grade: Camp Lebanon (a Baptist youth camp in Pennsylvania). God gave me seeds of faith and a vision of a better future.
- March 1980: heard and believed the gospel at Sandy Cove youth conference, although I did not begin to live as a Christian.
- July 1980: received Christ as Savior and Lord at Tuscarora Conference Center. God told me, in a very personal way, that he would use my life to make a difference in this world. My spiritual pilgrimage began in earnest.

- August 1990: God confirmed the call to writing. My first book contract with Focus on the Family.
- July 1993: spiritual gifts class. Understood why I see the world the way I do; understood the nature of my call to ministry.
- March 1996: Women of Virtue conference, Tucson, Arizona. God confirmed the call to speaking ministry.
- February 2000: overwhelmed with the love of God while sitting in my prayer room in Payson, Arizona.
- October 2004: Papua New Guinea. Received God's call to be a prophet to the nations.
- November 2005: life-altering pilgrimage to the Middle East.

We not only have biblical testimonies and our own stones of remembrance, but we also have the testimonies from all of church history. Few things have done more to bolster my faith than reading the biographies of great heroes of the faith. Their example convinces me that I, too, can experience the power of God. One of my favorites is *The Autobiography of George Müller,* which is his spiritual journal—his stones of remembrance—printed for all the world to read. What a blessing!

Of course, it's tempting to feel spiritually inferior when we read about the giants of church history. We think: *I wish I had lived during the days of John Wesley or the Welsh Revival. Too bad great revivals don't happen anymore.* However, God wants our remembering to strengthen and encourage us, not make us envious of days gone by. Besides, some of the most amazing revivals in church history are unfolding right *now* in places such as Columbia, Uganda, and China. Churches throughout Africa and Asia routinely report miracles similar to those recorded in the book of Acts: the lame walk, the blind see, the dead are raised back to life. You and I haven't missed out! Whatever God has done in ages past, he can and will do in our day. He can and will do in *your life*. You *can* experience his power.

Dear heavenly Father, thank you for prompting saints of old to record your faithful acts, so that we can learn and remember. Holy Spirit, help me to study and remember the testimonies of those people, then and now, who had the courage to believe you could do mighty things. Also bring to mind all the wonderful things you have done for me and those I love. Today, I raise stones of remembrance as a testimony to your faithfulness. Amen.

AFFIRM

I choose to remember the works of God.

APPLY

1. *What* does God want us to remember?

_____

_____

_____

2. *Why* does he want us to remember?

_____

_____

_____

3. Recount a testimony someone shared with you that had a powerful impact on your life.

_____

_____

_____

4. Recap one or more of your most significant stones of remembrance.

_____

_____

_____

5. Who are some people who might be either encouraged or challenged by your testimony? Write the names and which aspect of your story you want to share with them.

_____

_____

_____

_____

Act

1. Raise up some stones of remembrance. If you are willing, record these in the front of your Bible (or use a spiritual journal).
2. Spend time researching church history at www.chi.gospel com.net. Consider purchasing some of their documentaries, films, and other materials. You can also learn what God is doing around the world today by ordering the Transformation Videos (about past and present revivals around the world). Visit www.sentinelgroup.org.
3. Ask Christians you meet to tell you about the power of God in their lives. Discover firsthand how such testimonies help build power-packed faith!
4. Write out today's affirmation and scripture in your index-card notebook.
5. Write out your own prayer, expressing what God has shown you today about his mighty power.

_____

_____

_____

_____

Align Yourself with God's Purposes

I do nothing on my own.

JOHN 8:28

*I*f we want to experience the power of God in our lives, we need to be like Jesus, who always lived in alignment with the Father's purposes. We know little about Jesus's childhood other than he was born in a humble stable, lived in Egypt for a while (see Matthew 2:13–19), and taught some religious leaders in the temple when he was twelve years old (see Luke 2:41–50). We can assume these years were filled with preparation for his public ministry, because, as the gospel of Luke tells us, by age twelve, "Everyone who heard him was amazed at his understanding and his answers" (2:47) and "Jesus grew in wisdom and stature, and in favor with God and men" (2:52). We are told nothing more until Jesus, age thirty, turns up at the Jordan River to be baptized by John (see 3:21–23). We know he was studying Scripture, obeying his parents, learning carpentry, becoming wise, and enjoying favor.

After Jesus was baptized, "heaven was opened and the Holy Spirit descended on him in bodily form like a dove. And a voice came from heaven: 'You are my Son, whom I love; with you I am well pleased'" (3:21–22). The Holy Spirit immediately led Jesus into the desert, where he fasted forty days and endured a time of intense spiritual opposition. Luke explains what happened afterward: "Jesus returned to Galilee in the power of the Spirit, and news about him spread through the whole countryside" (4:14).

If Jesus had already actively demonstrated the power of God, it would not have been *news* when he "returned to Galilee in the power of the Spirit." Of course, the Bible doesn't tell us many things, but that doesn't mean they weren't true or didn't happen. However, there's no evidence that he exercised supernatural power prior to the launch of his public ministry. Instead, his first thirty years appear to have been a season of quiet preparation. Jesus stayed in alignment with the Father's wishes, whether that meant demonstrating or *refraining from demonstrating* power. Note, for example, that Jesus tells his mother (who was pressuring him to demonstrate power) that the timing wasn't right. If Jesus thought it essential that his demonstration of divine power be in alignment with the Father's purposes, how much more critical is knowing and embracing God's purposes for us?

I've often marveled at Jesus's remark, "I do nothing on my own" (John 8:28). The Son of God did nothing on his own, apart from the Father, yet we somehow think we can manufacture something spiritually powerful or eternally worthwhile on our own. Impossible! If Christ—the incarnate power of God—relied on the Father to tell him what to do, how much more do we need to walk in humble reliance? Like Jesus, we can only do what we see the Father doing. We must be in alignment with Father God—his purposes, priorities, and timing. We can't just go out into the world with our own agendas and ask God to bless whatever we feel like doing. In general, we shouldn't ask God to bless what we are doing; we should find out what God is doing and join him, because that activity or ministry is already blessed.

In the book of Acts, Peter and John heal a man at the Beautiful Gate (see 3:2–10). The man had been sitting at the gate for years. We can well imagine that Jesus walked right past him dozens, if not hundreds of times, but the man didn't experience the power of God *until the time was right*. The word rendered "Beautiful," *horaios,* means "the right hour." The power of God will only flow when a servant of God operates in alignment with God's purposes, priorities, and timing. This is extremely important to remember.

Let me give you a personal example that illustrates the importance of being in alignment with God's purposes. Right now, I'm experiencing tremendous neck pain. Of course, it's no mystery *why* my neck hurts. I've been slumping over typewriters and computer keyboards for almost thirty years. I've written twenty-two books, not to mention countless articles, a mountain of Internet content, and thousands of e-mails. My neck hurts as a direct result of my choices.

By contrast, my back doesn't hurt at all, and that is a miracle. Just hours ago, I left home to drive two hours to a retreat center to finish writing this book. Within minutes, a reckless driver cut me off on the freeway. In trying to avert an accident, I pulled so hard on the wheel that I pulled a muscle in my back.[2] Suddenly, the pain in my neck was nothing compared to the excruciating, searing pain in my back. I was literally screaming out in pain. Then panic gripped me: *How can I possibly keep driving, let alone meet my pressing deadline?* I called my ten-year-old daughter, Tara, and told her Mommy urgently needed prayer.

By the time I arrived at my destination, the pain in my back had vanished. But my neck was still throbbing. God miraculously healed my back in response to prayer…so why hasn't he healed my neck? In general, why does God heal some illnesses and not others? Why do we sometimes see God's miraculous intervention and sometimes not? That's a huge question, one we'll never entirely be able to answer this side of heaven. However, one thing is certain: God will do whatever advances *his* kingdom purposes. If that means healing—and in many cases it does—then he will bring healing, with or without a doctor's help.

But sometimes we don't experience healing until we address the underlying causes of the problem. I've been in healing services and, at the risk of offending someone, it was obvious to me that even if God miraculously healed their current problems, some of the people standing around the altar clearly needed to take better care of themselves, or they'd soon have another ailment requiring healing. Obesity, poor diet, lack of exercise, untamed emotions, and stress-dominated lifestyles are at the root of almost all degenerative diseases. While people who are significantly overweight may need to exercise their faith, what they really need is physical exercise.

God is not going to follow us around with a magic wand, waving away the consequences of our behavior. He won't routinely suspend the laws of sowing and reaping for our benefit. Yes, sometimes he intervenes and we witness a dramatic healing, but he's also given us words of wisdom and exhortation. Imagine what kind of people we would become if we could disobey God's direct commandments (including his command to purify ourselves of everything that contaminates body and spirit) and never suffer any negative results. After all, behavior that gets rewarded gets repeated. I would live on curly fries and Oreo milkshakes from Jack in the Box, and I'd never forgive anyone *ever*!

God can do whatever he wants. However, his miraculous power is most often demonstrated when we align ourselves with his purposes, walking in obedience. In averting that car accident, I was in alignment with God's will for me. My injury was not due to my own foolish choices; it occurred in a moment of wisdom as I veered away from oncoming traffic. So, in choosing to grant divine healing, God was not rewarding disobedience or foolishness.

By contrast, I believe he hasn't healed my neck because, in that area of my life, I am *not* in alignment with his purposes. I spend too many hours at the computer, neglecting other vital responsibilities, and I have failed to properly care for my body. My neck is a warning sign: if I want to be used by God for decades to come—and I do—then I better start walking in obedience, taking care of myself in spirit, soul, *and* body. I need to faithfully perform the stretching exercises my doctor has assigned, give heed to my office ergonomics, set reasonable working hours, and schedule routine physical therapy.

God's purposes included motivating me to take a long-term view of ministry, realizing the need to stay productive over the long haul, while at the same time teaching Tara that if she prays for the sick (or injured), she will see miracles! By healing my back, but not my neck, God accomplished both his purposes. Sometimes God empowers us to heal or be healed; other times he empowers us to walk in wisdom. Sometimes he gives us power enough for both. Whatever the case, his power is expressed as we align ourselves with his purposes. His power is expressed when we are obedient.

Although God didn't grant healing for my neck, he did demonstrate mercy. Within two minutes of arriving at the conference center, I met one of the other guests who was checking in at the same time. She mentioned that she was a massage therapist, and as we talked, she said, "God has just laid it on my heart to give you a massage tonight. What time would work for you?" I wrote for a few hours then experienced the most wonderful ninety-minute therapeutic massage in the comfort of my room. The therapist refused to let me pay, saying it was a gift from God through her.

Let's return to the Bible, where we see God's power in the life of Moses during those times when he was aligned with God's purposes. When he held up his staff and parted the Red Sea, he was exercising supernatural power to lead the Israelites to freedom. But when he tried to access that same supernatural power to settle all their disputes, God sent his father-in-law, Jethro, to say, "What you are doing is not good. You and these people who come to you will only wear yourselves out. The work is too heavy for you; you cannot handle it alone" (Exodus 18:17–18). In the first instance, Moses was in alignment with God's stated purpose of bringing the people out of Egypt. In the second case, Moses needed to get into alignment with God's desire for him to lead with wisdom. Although God didn't solve Moses's problem, he *did* in his mercy send someone who could help.

Experiencing God's power is not about getting God to align with our agendas; it is about getting in alignment with him. It is about walking in obedience.

~⌇

Dear heavenly Father, thank you for sending Jesus, not only to bring salvation to the world, but to show us how we might join our Triune God in the vital work of bringing that salvation into all the earth. I stand amazed that, because Christ Jesus lives in me, I can also experience the power of God flowing in and through my life. Holy Spirit, teach me to be sensitive to your leading so that I can perceive and join in your work. Amen.

ᗩFFIRM

If I want to experience God's power, I must align myself with his purposes.

ᗩPPLY

1. Can you think of an area in your life where you have *not* experienced God's power? Describe.

   _____

   _____

   _____

2. Reflect upon your answer to question 1. Is it possible that God hasn't intervened in your situation because you are out of alignment with his purposes?

   _____

   _____

   _____

3. Ask God to reveal his purposes in your situation. What are some practical steps you can take to get into alignment with God?

_____

_____

_____

4. Describe a time when you saw God's power demonstrated, and note how you were in alignment with his purposes at that time or in that situation.

_____

_____

_____

5. If it was important for Jesus to be in alignment with the Father's will and timing, what does that mean for you personally as you seek to experience the power of God?

_____

_____

_____

ACT

1. Drawing upon your answer to question 3 above, create an action plan that will enable you to get back into alignment with the purposes of God.

2. Write out today's affirmation and scripture in your index-card notebook.

3. Write out your own prayer, expressing what God has shown you today about his mighty power.

_____

_____

_____

_____

Cherish God's Power More Than Your Pet Sins

I cried out to him with my mouth;
his praise was on my tongue.
If I had cherished sin in my heart,
the Lord would not have listened;
but God has surely listened
and heard my voice in prayer.

PSALM 66:17–19

*A*lthough this is painful for me, I feel it's important to tell a caution-
ary tale from my own life. A number of years ago, I completed a
forty-day fast, which was the most powerful experience of my life. I have
never felt better physically, never been sharper mentally or stronger spiritually. My relationships overflowed with love and peace. I prayed for and
with almost everyone, everywhere I went.

My impetus for fasting was the news that a friend, the mother of three
small children, had been diagnosed with cancer—multiple ovarian tumors
and a brain tumor. Like everyone else, I promised to pray for her. But I

felt so powerless. The Bible says, "The prayer of a righteous man is powerful and effective" (James 5:16), but my prayers were not powerful or effective. Of course, my powerless prayers had long been a source of frustration, but now the stakes were high enough that powerless prayers just weren't tolerable anymore.

Have you ever felt that way? Have you ever faced an impossible situation in which you thought, *If only I could pray for this person with confidence that my prayers will be answered.* Have you ever come face to face with a situation where nothing but the power of God could help—yet that power eluded you? Maybe that's where you are today, and it's why you picked up this book.

In desperation, I dropped to my knees and cried out to God, "I'll do whatever you ask of me, whatever it takes, but I've got to see your power at work." I had thought about completing a forty-day fast for many years; now, finally, I had the motivation to do it. Never have I prayed with such passion; never have I knocked so relentlessly on heaven's door—and never had I seen God move so dramatically. He healed my friend completely. I also saw him work on behalf of two other women. One was told she probably had cervical cancer. After prayer, subsequent tests delivered a clean bill of health. The other woman was told she had something suspicious-looking in her breast. I prayed for her, and soon afterward the radiologist dubbed the mammogram results a "mistake." While a skeptic may say these women never had cancer to begin with, I believe God intervened in their lives in answer to prayer.

God also showed up powerfully at events where I was speaking during this forty-day period. In several cities, pockets of revival broke out. When I prayed for people, God seemed to give me precisely the right words. Women were instantly set free from drugs, alcohol, cigarettes, and sexual addictions. It's been encouraging to hear reports from these women and from their ministry leaders that years later they continue to walk in

freedom. One woman launched a ministry to others struggling with homo-
sexuality; another is actively ministering to pregnant teens.

In addition, a summer-evening teaching series at my home church in
Phoenix attracted nearly two thousand people. (Unless you've been to the
desert in the summer, you have no idea how miraculous *that is*, as half the
population disappears!) Throughout the series, God was speaking to me
and through me. Everyone marveled at the powerful presence of God in
the sanctuary, and I even felt his power flowing through my hands as I laid
them on people, praying for them.

Then right around that time, someone profoundly wounded me.
The details are unimportant. What's important to tell you is that I han-
dled the situation very, very badly. My heart and mind were overcome
with pain. No matter how many times I tried to forgive the person,
somehow I would always crawl back to nursing and rehearsing the wrong
done to me. Not an hour went by that I didn't think about my wounds.
I couldn't sleep at night, tormented by bitterness. I struggled to function,
and my work suffered. No one could get within a mile of me without
hearing about how I'd been hurt. Friends, family, and spiritual leaders
kept warning me to let it go, but somehow I just couldn't. Or should I
say wouldn't?

I didn't realize how much it was costing me until my whole life came
crashing down around me. No words can describe the spiritual, emotional, and financial devastation my family and I experienced as a result.
For a long time, I told myself that one woman was the cause of these problems. But time at the feet of Jesus has shown me I was wrong. She had not
stopped the flow of the power of God in my life; my *sinful reaction* to her
had robbed me of the power of God.

My hurt, anger, bitterness, and resentment had defiled me—not to
mention everyone around me who had to listen to me. I had grieved the

Holy Spirit, so the power of God stopped flowing through my life. The anointing left. The joy and peace left. Just like that. My prayers no longer had the power to move God. My heart broke. I slipped into depression and began running to food for comfort. I gained thirty pounds and, after having proclaimed worldwide how the power of God had delivered me from being an emotional wreck, I went back on antidepressants, because I despaired of life.

Even now, my heart aches as I share this story. But you need to know that the power of God is not like a magic wand. It's not a permanent gift or, as they used to say on *Wheel of Fortune*, "Once you buy a prize, it's yours to keep." It flows from our relationship with God. Even if we have aligned ourselves with God's purposes, if we choose to wallow in sin, God steps back and says, *If that's what you truly want, have at it. But you can't have your sin and my power at the same time.* Or as King David put it: "If I had cherished sin in my heart, the Lord would not have listened" (Psalm 66:18).

David knew all about cherishing sin. This man after God's own heart cherished his sin with Bathsheba so much that he had her husband killed in order to keep his little secret. It wasn't until the prophet Nathan confronted David about his adultery that he was finally willing to repent. David also knew the joy of forgiveness and restoration that's available when a person is willing to come clean before God. He wrote:

> *Blessed is he*
> *whose transgressions are forgiven,*
> *whose sins are covered.*
> *Blessed is the man*
> *whose sin the LORD does not count against him*
> *and in whose spirit is no deceit.*

When I kept silent,
    my bones wasted away
    through my groaning all day long.
For day and night
    your hand was heavy upon me;
my strength was sapped
    as in the heat of summer.
Then I acknowledged my sin to you
    and did not cover up my iniquity.
I said, "I will confess
    my transgressions to the LORD"—
and you forgave
    the guilt of my sin. (Psalm 32:1–5)

God wants to work in and through our lives. He wants us to know the joy of winning victories in exciting spiritual battles as we experience his power. However, God *will* put us on the sidelines when we become contaminated by sin. That was true for me in the above situation. God eventually arranged circumstances, during which I had no choice but to come face to face with my sinful reactions to the hurt done to me. I began as an innocent victim but ended up someone who was victimizing others by subjecting them to my bitterness.

If you aren't experiencing God's power, something similar may have happened to you. Maybe someone hurt you. Maybe you've been hurt, over and over again, by a long succession of people. You haven't committed some grievous sin, but you have held on to your hurt and become bitter or angry or jealous or full of self-pity. Unfortunately, it doesn't stop there. If you're like most people, anyone who gets within a mile of you will be contaminated too, as your anger, bitterness, or jealousy rubs off on everyone you touch.

The good news is that God offers restoration if we are willing to humble ourselves. For me, it has been a long, painful process. I pray that I will never again cherish my sin more than I cherish the presence and power of God. At any point, we can throw up our hands and say, "My way isn't working. As much as I love my pet sins, it's just not worth it. I'd rather experience the power of God." At that moment of repentance, God will immediately set to work, purifying our hearts so that we can once again be vessels fit for his use.

Dear heavenly Father, please forgive me for cherishing my sin more than I cherish your presence and power. Please show me those things in my life that are preventing me from experiencing all the blessings you intend. My sincere desire is to be cleansed and fit for any good work. I invite you, Holy Spirit, to show me any area of my life that requires realignment. Amen.

AFFIRM

The power of God flows most consistently through pure vessels.

Apply

1. Have you ever been confronted with a situation where the only possible solution required the power of God? Describe the situation.

_____

_____

_____

2. How did you respond?

_____

_____

3. What was the final outcome of that situation? (If you are facing it right now, what is the current outcome?)

_____

_____

_____

4. Is there something you cherish more than the power of God?

_____

_____

_____

5. What would it take to drive you to your knees, declaring, "Whatever it takes, I need to experience the power of God?" If you are there right now, describe what has brought you to this place.

_____

_____

_____

ACT

1. Take specific steps to resolve anything that may be hindering the power of God in your life. If it's sin, confess it. If you've hurt someone, write a note, pick up the phone, schedule an appointment, and make it right. If you've been hurt, walk the painful path to forgiveness.
2. Write out today's affirmation and scripture in your index-card notebook.
3. Write out your own prayer, expressing what God has shown you today about his mighty power.

_____

_____

_____

_____

Don't Let a Guilty
Conscience Hold You Back

*If we confess our sins, he is faithful and
just and will forgive us our sins and
purify us from all unrighteousness.*

1 JOHN 1:9

$\mathcal{R}$achel had dropped out of sight again.
You couldn't help but notice her absence, even in a one-thousand-member congregation. Beautiful, vivacious, talented beyond reason. No one could decide if Rachel was more gifted as a worship leader, soloist, or Bible teacher. She had it all and could do it all. She ministered to teens, seniors, and prisoners with equal ease.

But now she was gone, and the void she left was palpable. This had been a pattern all her adult life—this appearing-disappearing-reappearing act. Rachel had a secret: prescription drugs. The habit started right after a car accident in college, when the doctor gave her a pain killer. She noticed it killed more than the physical pain; it covered the emotional hurt inflicted by her verbally abusive mother. Through the years, Rachel had visited many doctors for a variety of ailments, and each time she walked away with more prescriptions. Some pills calmed her down; others picked her up. Soon, she had a smorgasbord of medications to choose from and enough different doctors and pharmacists that no one knew what Rachel was up to. Except Rachel.

Depending upon which pills she decided to take, Rachel could keep up the happy front. But only for a while. She'd learned through the years that what goes up must come down. No matter how hard she tried, how many prayers she prayed or tears she shed, she eventually always came crashing down. The guilt and self-condemnation would become all consuming. A hate-filled inner voice would accuse: *How dare you show your face at church.* Then she'd crawl into what she called her cave—buried under the covers in her darkened bedroom, unable to get up even to drink a glass of water. The pattern had cost her more than one marriage.

Things had been bad before, but never this bad and for this long. Rachel had always managed to control her addiction—or so she thought. Her countless years spent self-medicating and managing her own biochemistry could have qualified her for a PhD. But her methods weren't working anymore. She was out of control. How could she ever face all those people at church who looked up to her? She felt so guilty.

Finally, Rachel knew the time had come. Week after week, she had seen the bulletin announcement for Celebrate Recovery,[3] the twelve-step program offered at the church on Monday nights. Until now, attending had never been an option. Not for Rachel. Beautiful, gifted, in-charge Rachel. Celebrate Recovery was for all those weak people, and she wasn't one of them. No way. She wasn't about to lower herself to that level. She didn't have to. The drugs did it for her. She had hit the infamous rock bottom.

"Walking into that room was the hardest thing I've ever done," she recalls. "I had walked past that door a million times, on my way to teach, to lead, to show the world how far I'd come. I had been a powerhouse in that church; now I had to admit just how powerless I really was. But when I finally confessed my sin, finally stopped trying to hide the truth, I felt liberated. I didn't have to run and hide in shame anymore. I could move forward with God, knowing he had forgiven me completely—not just for the mistakes I'd made long ago, but for the addiction that haunted my steps."

Once Rachel confessed her powerlessness, she opened her life to the power of God, and he delivered her from a twenty-year addiction to prescription drugs. That was years ago. Today, Rachel leads Celebrate Recovery in her church.

Like Rachel, if we want God's power to flow in us and through us, we have to come clean before God—and others. The Bible says, "Therefore confess your sins to each other and pray for each other so that you may be healed. The prayer of a righteous man is powerful and effective" (James 5:16). If we want our lives to be powerful and effective, we have to confess those sins we've committed once and those sins we battle daily. We'll never experience God's power while we are held captive to the power of something else: drugs, alcohol, the Internet, food, pride, bitterness, whatever.

One of the first Bible verses I memorized was 1 John 1:9. I knew I had a lot of sins to confess, having been picked up by the police on numerous occasions for everything from shoplifting to indecent exposure. Although I recited the verse many times, it took a long time before it dawned on me that it contains the word *and*, because it's talking about two distinct things God does when we confess our sins:

1. Forgives us our sins. That's one thing, *and*…
2. Purifies us from all unrighteousness.

It's important to understand the difference between forgiveness and purification. In the Old Testament, two different types of rituals prepared the Israelites to enter into the presence of God: sacrifices, which brought forgiveness, and ritual bathing or cleansing, which brought purification. Sacrifices dealt with the fact of sin; purifications dealt with the aftereffects of sin. A sacrifice was offered *on behalf of sinners* by the priest; purification was offered *to sinners* so they could feel clean again.

In the same way Christ offered himself as a sacrifice *on behalf of sinners* to deal with the fact of sin. He also made the Holy Spirit available *to sinners* so that we could experience the joy of spiritual purification. This purifying makes us *feel clean again*, addressing the aftermath of sin. We need both forgiveness and purification in order to live in freedom. If you are a Christian, you have been declared "not guilty" in God's sight. Therefore, you shouldn't *feel* guilty: "The blood of goats and bulls and the ashes of a heifer sprinkled on those who are ceremonially unclean sanctify them so that they are outwardly clean. How much more, then, will the blood of Christ, who through the eternal Spirit offered himself unblemished to God, cleanse our consciences" (Hebrews 9:13–14).

Unfortunately, many Christians whom God has declared "not guilty" live beaten-down lives, heads hung in shame, believing a pack of lies about how God can't use them anymore. But Jesus died so we could live free from a guilty conscience (see Hebrews 10:22). Do you know why priests in the Old Testament were sprinkled with blood? So that they could *serve* God in the temple. We are supposed to serve God here on earth in this temple, in this earthen vessel—ourselves. Hebrews 9:14 tells us the reason it's so important to have our consciences cleansed: "*so that* we may serve the living God!" (emphasis added).

Think about it for a minute: Why don't people serve God? Why don't they step out in ministry? Often because they don't think they're good enough. There's a little CD playing in their heads, reciting a never-ending litany of sins and shortcomings. Although the slate has been washed clean in heaven, it hasn't been washed clean in their heads. God wants us to be *free* of guilt and to *feel free* of guilt so we can serve him.

But that can be a difficult thing to receive for many of us. It certainly was for Naaman, and his story can give us some insight into how we can become vessels that God can use. We find the story in 2 Kings 5.

Naaman, a commander in the army of Aram, was sidelined because the disease of leprosy had contaminated him. Although he'd had many military victories, Naaman couldn't be on active duty for his king because he might contaminate others who came in contact with him.

A servant, who was a captive from Israel, told Naaman's wife that Elisha could heal Naaman of his leprosy. "So Naaman went with his horses and chariots and stopped at the door of Elisha's house. Elisha sent a messenger to say to him, 'Go, wash yourself seven times in the Jordan, and your flesh will be restored and you will be cleansed'" (verses 9–10).

When Naaman heard what Elisha had said, he was *furious*. He said, "I thought that he would surely come out to me and stand and call on the name of the LORD his God, wave his hand over the spot and cure me of my leprosy. Are not Abana and Pharpar, the rivers of Damascus, better than any of the waters of Israel? Couldn't I wash in them and be cleansed?" (verses 11–12).

Naaman was angry for many reasons:

- He had his own ideas about what it would take and what it would look like to experience the power of God. Notice he says, "I thought…," and describes in specific detail how he expected everything to unfold. That same attitude gets us all in trouble! We think we know better than God.
- He was looking for something dramatic; God was looking for humble obedience.

- Naaman wanted someone else (namely Elisha) to do something that would enable him to experience God's power (for example, call on God or wave his hand); he didn't want to have to take action himself. This is a common mistake we all make. People want to attend a big conference with a famous Christian and have *that person* do something, whether it's praying for them or anointing them with oil. God wanted Naaman to take a step of faith for himself so he could experience the power of God directly. The same is true for us.

Fortunately, Naaman's story has a happy ending. He was cleansed and restored when he took a step of faith in obedience to God's command to wash and be cleansed. We can follow in his footsteps by taking the step outlined in 1 John 1:9, believing by faith that God will do as he says—forgive us and purify us.

God wants us, like Naaman, to experience that glorious moment when we lift up our purified hands and say, "I'm ready to get back to work in service to my king. I'm ready to see God's power flowing through my life again."

God created us to walk with joy and a healthy God-confidence. Although he never promised that the circumstances of life would always go our way, he has placed within us the power to rise above life's challenges rather than be constantly defeated, discouraged, and frustrated. He has given us an ever-present solution for those times when we aren't experiencing his power in our lives because of a guilty conscience: confession, which brings about our purification. Once we confess our sins, we are forgiven and cleansed, and his power can flow in and through us once again. Just a trickle at first, but as we continue to abide in him, eventually we will have a mighty rushing river. That's his promise.

*Dear heavenly Father, thank you for understanding me so well,
far better than I understand myself. I want to be used by you, to
demonstrate your power to hurting people. But I just don't feel good
enough. The weight of my sins and shortcomings holds me back.
Thank you for providing purification as a gift to set me free from
the burden of my guilty conscience. Holy Spirit, teach me how to
lead a life of continual confession and cleansing, so that I'm always
ready to be of service to my King. In Jesus's name. Amen.*

AFFIRM

Confession and cleansing set me free to serve God.

APPLY

1. What has God provided to deal with the sin in your life?

   _____

   _____

   _____

2. What has God provided to deal with the guilty feelings associated with sin?

_____

_____

_____

3. Describe a time when you were held back from serving God because of a guilty conscience.

_____

_____

_____

4. As you allow God to cleanse you from sin, express how the purifying power of the Holy Spirit impacts both your emotions and your willingness to serve God.

_____

_____

_____

_____

5. What was the most significant lesson you learned from the life of Naaman?

_____

_____

_____

ACT

1. Set aside time to wash and be cleansed. You can do this alone, with your family, or with a small group. (Notice that Naaman was cleansed publicly, so please pray about doing this ceremony with at least a few others.) Obtain a pitcher of water, an empty basin, and a hand towel. Kneel quietly, asking God to bring to mind anything that might be contaminating you, whether it's your own sins or your sinful response to people and/or circumstances. Confess these aloud, asking God to both forgive you and purify you. Wash your hands, then lift them up, offering them again in service to your God and king.

   Of course, there is nothing mystical about this cleansing ceremony. It does not make you spiritually clean. Instead, it is intended to give you a tangible encounter with a spiritual reality: *you are cleansed through confession.* I have conducted this ceremony all over the world, always with powerful results. I believe it will be a blessing to you.

2. Write out today's affirmation and scripture in your index-card notebook.

3. Write out your own prayer, expressing what God has shown you today about his mighty power.

Commit to Daily Confession and Repentance

*Jesus stood and said in a loud voice, "If anyone
is thirsty, let him come to me and drink.
Whoever believes in me, as the Scripture has said,
streams of living water will flow from within him."*

JOHN 7:37–38

*M*y prayer is that yesterday's cleansing ceremony was a powerfully healing time for you. However, purification is not a one-time event. It's a way of life. It must be daily. Cleansing must precede service, even if that service is something as simple as praying for a friend. Before praying for anyone, I bow my head and quietly ask God if anything in my life needs to be washed away that would hinder my ability to be a conduit for God's power.

Every day junk comes into our lives that can pollute our spirits, stopping the flow of those "streams of living water" that Jesus spoke about. In Old Testament times, people deliberately polluted water and stopped up wells as an act of warfare. For example, the book of Genesis tells us that "[Isaac] had so many flocks and herds and servants that the Philistines envied him. So all the wells that his father's servants had dug in the time of his father Abraham, the Philistines stopped up, filling them with earth" (Genesis 26:14–15). To this day, the devil uses a similar tactic in his war against us. He works overtime to contaminate us and stop the flow of God's power in us. While he might tempt us with drugs, alcohol, gambling, or sexual addictions in his efforts to pollute us, he's just as likely to tempt us to gossip, complain, criticize, and condemn others— and all the while we're congratulating ourselves for being such good Christians.

If we want to be fit and ready for God to work through us, we must remain alert to the devil's attempts to stop the flow of God's power in our lives. The Bible tells us what a "flowing" life looks like: "love, joy, peace, patience, kindness, goodness, faithfulness, gentleness, and self-control" (Galatians 5:22–23). The simplest way to know whether we're flowing or stopped up is to listen in on our own conversations, because "out of the overflow of the heart the mouth speaks" (Matthew 12:34). Listen to the silent conversation that runs through your mind. Do love, joy, and all those wonderful attributes characterize your thoughts and conversations… or are you constantly finding fault with everyone and everything, while adamantly defending yourself?

If we want to unleash God's power in our lives, we must be aware of those people or situations that tempt us to abandon love, joy, peace, and the other fruit of the Spirit—those times when someone hurts our feelings, does us wrong, or drags us into an interpersonal conflict.[4] We need to be watchful of such people and situations, because they can effectively block the flow of God's power if we are not careful to maintain a pure heart. It helps to remind ourselves: people aren't the real enemy; often, they are just tools in the hands of our true Enemy. "Our struggle is not against flesh and blood, but against the rulers, against the authorities, against the powers of this dark world and against the spiritual forces of evil in the heavenly realms" (Ephesians 6:12).

We shouldn't limit our vigilance to those times when things aren't going our way. We need to be careful that the power is flowing even when things *are going our way.* Notice that according to Genesis, the Philistines stopped up Isaac's well when his life was at its best. He was prospering in every way, thanks in no small measure to the efforts of his father, Abraham. When things come easily for us, when we're flowing along, serving in the church, our pride can stop the flow of God's power. We may be too hard on others, wondering why they can't live the "victorious Christian life" as well as we do. Or we may get complacent, thinking we've arrived spiritually. Or it might happen that when others see us believing our own press, they make it their business to take us down a notch or two. And maybe that's for the best.

In his outstanding book *Returning to Holiness,* Dr. Gregory Frizzell notes, "Unfortunately, in today's highly programmed church, deep spiritual cleansing is either ignored entirely or quickly glossed over in a surface manner. As a result, God's people are largely unaware of the subtle, unconfessed sins that daily quench Christ's full power in their lives.... An uncleansed heart is certainly why many believers battle spiritual weariness and lack God's mountain-moving power."[5]

God is both able and eager to work through our lives in powerful ways, but our sin separates us from him:

> *Surely the arm of the LORD is not too short to save,*
> *nor his ear too dull to hear.*
> *But your iniquities have separated*
> *you from your God;*
> *your sins have hidden his face from you,*
> *so that he will not hear. (Isaiah 59:1–2)*

If our prayers aren't answered, the problem is never with God. Bottom line: God can't answer prayers that he can't hear. A life of unanswered prayer is a powerless life. It's just that simple. If you want to become a vessel of God's power, daily confession and repentance is absolutely essential. Don't be afraid of the process. God only reveals what he is ready to heal, and since he created you, he knows when you're ready to take the next step on your own journey to holiness. So invite the Holy Spirit to show you the truth about your heart's condition. Set aside time at the end of each day to reflect.

Dr. Frizzell offers these very practical areas to consider.[6]

SINS OF THOUGHT

Reflect on what you've been thinking about. Do your thoughts line up with Philippians 4:8: "Whatever is true, whatever is noble, whatever is right, whatever is pure, whatever is lovely, whatever is admirable—if anything is excellent or praiseworthy—think about such things"? Ask the Holy Spirit to bring to remembrance any thoughts that were untrue, ignoble, wrong, impure, unlovely, negative, or destructive. You will probably notice sinful thought patterns. It's tempting to dismiss our sinful thoughts as no big deal. To say, "It's not like I'm *doing* anything wrong." But that's not the biblical perspective. Proverbs 23:7 tells us, "As [a man] thinketh in his heart, so is he" (KJV). Thoughts inevitably lead to actions, as surely as night follows day. Let God cleanse those thoughts before they come to fruition.

Also consider this helpful exercise. For one twenty-four-hour period make a note, every hour, about how you've occupied your mind. Were you thinking about the things of God? Or at the very least, were you thinking positive, constructive thoughts? Many of us constantly think about ourselves, especially what's wrong with us, then wonder why our lives aren't power-packed. If they remain unconfessed, sins of thought block God's power in our lives.

SINS OF ATTITUDE

Do you have an attitude problem? The Bible says, "Do nothing out of selfish ambition or vain conceit, but in humility consider others better than yourselves. Each of you should look not only to your own interests, but also to the interests of others. Your attitude should be the same as that of Christ Jesus" (Philippians 2:3–5). Given that definition, we *all* have an attitude problem. Are you routinely frustrated with or impatient toward others? If so, you have an underlying attitude problem. It's the insidious problem of pride. You think you're better, smarter, faster, more insightful, whatever. God warns us that he "opposes the proud but gives grace to the humble" (1 Peter 5:5). Something tells me Peter, in particular, knew what it meant for God to oppose him. I wonder how often Christians tell themselves, "The devil is opposing me," when it's God himself who is opposing them because of their pride—their crummy, self-centered attitude.

Another attitude to guard against is unforgiveness. It's possible to have an ongoing tendency *not* to forgive but, instead, to hold on to hurts, keeping a record of wrongs. Our attitude needs to be loving, because love "keeps no record of wrongs" (1 Corinthians 13:5). Rather than let hurts and hard feelings pile up, clean the slate daily.

SINS OF SPEECH

This is the hardest area for me. Speaking is my gift, but my mouth also gets me into more trouble than you can imagine! How different our lives would be if we could live up to this one sentence in the Bible: "Do not let any unwholesome talk come out of your mouths, but only what is helpful for building others up according to their needs, that it may benefit those who listen" (Ephesians 4:29). This verse speaks to us in black and white, not gray, terms. It's absolute: *no* unwholesome talk. Who is equal to the task? Only perfect people: "If anyone is never at fault in what he says, he is a perfect man, able to keep his whole body in check" (James 3:2). Jesus was the only perfect man who ever lived. So the rest of us had better check what comes off our tongues—*daily.*

Areas to reflect upon at the end of each day include: arguing, complaining, gossiping, criticizing, judging, slandering, lying, exaggerating, cursing, and making off-color comments. Pray over each person you encountered and the conversations you had throughout the day. Is there anything you need to confess to God? Do you need to ask anyone's forgiveness? As you take time to confess sins of speech, you may grow to the point that you check your words before they leave your mouth. Wouldn't that be ideal? As you confess sins of speech, ask God to empower you for the days to come: "Set a guard over my mouth, O LORD; keep watch over the door of my lips" (Psalm 141:3). That's a prayer request God is eager to answer. It would also be helpful to routinely meditate upon James 3:1–12, which reminds us to tame our tongues.

SINS OF RELATIONSHIPS

No one can make you sin; but other people certainly have a way of bringing our sin to the surface, don't they! I often say, "I can get along fine when it's just me and God. It's only when *people* come around that I get into trouble!" The toughest command of all is to love our neighbors—including those we consider enemies—as we love ourselves. Again, from a purely human perspective, this is impossible. However, last night I was reading about Coptic Christians living in Egypt under the rule of the Roman

Empire. As these believers were being tortured to death, they forgave their executioners. I also read about a Ugandan pastor targeted for death by former dictator Idi Amin. The pastor asked his killers if he could pray before he died—not for himself (after all, he knew he'd be with Jesus in a few minutes) but for *them.*

Like it or not, God says how we treat people *matters to him.* He says, in essence, *don't bother talking to me until you can get along with one another.* As the apostle John put it, "If anyone says, 'I love God,' yet hates his brother, he is a liar. For anyone who does not love his brother, whom he has seen, cannot love God, whom he has not seen. And he has given us this command: Whoever loves God must also love his brother" (1 John 4:20–21). We're just fooling ourselves if we ignore this, but God is not fooled, and he will not unleash his power in us if we persist in our unloving ways. That's why Jesus said, "If you are offering your gift at the altar and there remember that your brother has something against you, leave your gift there in front of the altar. First go and be reconciled to your brother; then come and offer your gift" (Matthew 5:23–24).

Do you need to be reconciled with anyone? Maybe you're holding on to an old, old injury, and you have to track that person down to ask forgiveness. One of the most powerful movies I've ever seen was *The Straight Story,* which chronicles a trip made by seventy-three-year-old Alvin Straight from Laurens, Iowa, to Mount Zion, Wisconsin, in 1994. He had lost his driver's license due to failing eyesight, so he rode a 1966 John Deere *lawn mower* 260 miles, through rain and every conceivable obstacle. His mission? To be reconciled to his estranged seventy-five-year-old brother, Lyle, who had suffered a stroke. If you are lacking God's power in your life—and you know you have a significant issue with someone—look no further for an explanation to the mystery. "First go and be reconciled to your brother." Even if it means riding 260 miles on a lawn mower. Do it.

It's also a good policy to make sure you are reconciled to everyone in your immediate family before going to bed each night. Take seriously the biblical admonition: "Do not let the sun go down while you are still angry" (Ephesians 4:26). Visit each bedroom before you sleep and clear the air. You'll not only sleep better, you'll also unleash the power of God in your life.

Sins of Commission and Sins of Omission

Everyone can relate to the apostle Paul's frustration when he cried out, "I do not understand what I do. For what I want to do I do not do, but what I hate I do" (Romans 7:15). We all struggle with sins of commission— things we do that we know we shouldn't do, and sins of omission—things we fail to do even though we know we should. As a child growing up in the Catholic Church, I learned a prayer of confession that has stayed with me all my life. Perhaps it will help you as well:

Act of Contrition

O my God, I am heartily sorry
For having offended Thee,
and I detest all my sins,
because of thy just punishments
but most all because they offend Thee, my God
Who art all good and deserving of all my love.
I firmly resolve, with the help of Thy grace
to sin no more and to avoid the near occasions of sin. Amen.[7]

Most of us have a good idea of what we're doing—or failing to do—that grieves the heart of God. Perhaps we don't pray, or maybe we are withholding our tithe, neglecting God's Word, or abusing our bodies by failing to eat right and exercise. If you are grieving God's heart, the Holy Spirit will reveal it to you. Bring whatever he shows you before your gracious Father, asking him to cleanse your heart and give you a fresh start the next morning.

Unleashing God's power in your life requires a commitment to daily confession and repentance. Set aside time each evening to examine yourself using Dr. Frizzell's guidelines. If the power of God is not flowing through your life, if you are not routinely seeing answers to prayer, you probably need to confess your sins and be cleansed. Make it a daily habit.

Dear heavenly Father, I'm so thankful your power is available both to me and through me. I stand in awe at the realization that you've commissioned me to play a vital part in seeing your kingdom come and your will done on this earth. I want your streams of living water to flow through my life. Holy Spirit, teach me to be alert to those things that stop up my well. Make me teachable—quick to repent and quick to forgive. I confess that, in the past, I've blamed you for the lack of power in my life. I want to live a life of continual confession, so that nothing will hinder you from working in and through me. Amen.

AFFIRM

The power of God will keep flowing as long as I am purified daily.

APPLY

1. What evidence is there that something is blocking God's power in your life?

   _____

   _____

   _____

2. What types of people or situations tend to fill your well with mud and rocks?

   _____

   _____

   _____

3. How can you be more alert to the types of things that stop up the flow of God in your life? Be as practical as possible.

_____

_____

_____

4. Describe a time when your well was stopped up and/or a time when you were purified and noted a dramatic change in the flow of God's power.

_____

_____

_____

5. How will you incorporate a time of daily cleansing into your routine?

_____

_____

_____

ACT

1. Consider using your daily shower or bath as a time to cleanse spirit, soul, and body, confessing your sins and forgiving those who have sinned against you. Another great time to clean the slate is as you say good night to each of your loved ones.
2. Take some extended time today to pray over each area of sin.
3. Write out today's affirmation and scripture in your index-card notebook.

4. Write out your own prayer, expressing what God has shown you today about his mighty power.

_____

_____

_____

_____

Pursue a Lifestyle of Radical Purity

Since we have these promises, dear friends, let us purify
ourselves from everything that contaminates body and
spirit, perfecting holiness out of reverence for God.

2 CORINTHIANS 7:1

When Tina Marie was ten years old, she began praying for her future husband. She even made a deal with God. She recalls, "I would remain pure until my wedding night as long as God didn't come back for his people before I got married!" It hasn't been an easy road in a culture that bombards people with sexual temptations—especially in the circles Tina Marie has traveled. Although she grew up on a Midwestern dairy farm, shortly after college she moved to Hollywood, where she was surrounded by handsome models and actors. She has been a guest on numerous television shows, appeared in movies, commercials, and music videos. Yet even in the midst of the glamour and temptation, Tina's commitment to purity remained strong. In fact, it grew.

Tina had a profound sense of calling—not only to protect her purity, but to challenge others to do the same. She decided the best way to spread the abstinence message was through the Miss America pageant, which would give her credibility and a national platform. She competed in a preliminary contest for the title of Miss Los Angeles and was chosen to model evening gowns at the Miss America pageant in Atlantic City in September 2001. When she didn't win the crown that night, Tina Marie knew her hopes of becoming Miss America had been dashed. She was already older than most of the contestants, so she knew her time had passed. She thought her dream of being God's messenger to promote purity was over too.

Later that night, she went to walk alone along the boardwalk. Now she was questioning both God's call on her life and her own commitment. She wanted to throw it all away; to walk into a dance club and go with the first guy who paid attention to her. Suddenly, she heard a loud, commanding voice behind her. But when she turned, she saw only an old homeless man. The moment is etched in her memory forever, "He locked eyes with me and said, 'You *must* save your virginity! God *will honor* your decision and give you everything you've always wanted and much more. You must wait! Save yourself until your wedding night.'"

Without thinking, she yelled back at him, "I will! I promise!" She walked a few more steps in shock, then turned around…and the old man was gone. "I knew at that moment God had sent me an angel. I renewed my commitment that night to remain a virgin until my wedding night, and I have maintained my purity. Today, at twenty-nine, I'm engaged to an amazing Christ-filled man, and we will join forces to do ministry together. God has blessed me more than I could have ever imagined—just as he promised."

Today, Tina Marie speaks to thousands of teens and parents throughout the world about her abstinence pledge and how the media twists the truth. Her firsthand experience in Hollywood and her knowledge of what really goes on behind the scenes is an eyeopener—and downright infuriating! I had the privilege of speaking alongside Tina to hundreds of teens, and believe me, God is using her to demonstrate his power.[8]

Tina Marie and her fiancé were recently featured on an ABC morning talk show, and her work continues to garner secular media attention. She says, "Pop culture glamorizes life-threatening behaviors without showing the consequences, and it is my lifelong commitment to expose their lies and speak God's truth. The messages the media promotes destroy millions of lives worldwide. The people involved need to take responsibility for that. Meanwhile, I'm on a mission to warn people not to believe what the pop culture feeds them on a daily basis. Purity is the only way because it's God's way."

I believe God is calling his people to walk in his power, perhaps in ways unprecedented in church history. And God's sworn Enemy, Satan, knows that a key to power is purity. That's why the forces of darkness have launched an all-out offensive of impurity: filth on television, filth on the Internet, filth in magazines and films. Yet many Christians are no longer shocked or offended by photos of scantily clad women and by headlines touting the latest sex technique. We have become blinded to our own impurity and hardened in our hearts.

Yet Scripture makes it plain that if we want to be ready for *any* good work, we've got to be purified. Paul wrote:

> So whoever cleanses himself [from what is ignoble and unclean, who separates himself from contact with contaminating and corrupting influences] will [then himself] be a vessel set apart and useful for honorable and noble purposes, consecrated and profitable to the Master, fit and ready for any good work.
> (2 Timothy 2:21, AMP)

God is *willing* to work though anyone who is *willing;* but that willingness must be sincere, and it must be demonstrated. Lip service isn't enough. God looks at the heart, yes, but "out of the overflow of the heart the mouth speaks" (Matthew 12:34). The proof is in our lifestyles. It doesn't matter what we say; what we do gives us away every time.

God can do whatever he wants through whomever he chooses. I wrote a book, *Becoming a Vessel God Can Use,* around the premise that God often chooses the most unlikely people to accomplish his eternal purposes. However, I would be doing you a disservice if I didn't share my conviction that you are highly unlikely to experience God's power in significant ways if you are living the typical Western lifestyle, featuring a hectic daily schedule capped off with three hours of television viewing and/or Internet surfing, during which you're deluged with impure messages. All things are possible, but some things are highly improbable.

God has commanded us to purify ourselves of everything that contaminates body and spirit. We have to make a choice for purity, because the default in today's world is defilement. Just yesterday, one of my friends discovered that her husband is addicted to Internet pornography, has been visiting prostitutes, and, worst of all, came dangerously close to an affair with his best friend's wife. If that's not shocking enough, here's the kicker: this man is a highly regarded spiritual leader who sincerely loves God. He started down the slippery slope to impurity by clicking a button on his computer one day and flirting "innocently" on another day. He wasn't committed to a lifestyle of radical purity, and that lack of commitment was all the devil needed to get a foothold, thus effectively stopping the flow of God's power in and through this Christian leader.

Contrast this contemporary example with the example of Joseph in Scripture. He was so committed to a lifestyle of radical purity that when his master's wife tried to seduce him, "he...ran out of the house" (Genesis 39:12), knowing there would be grave consequences for disobeying her. He preferred prison to impurity. That's what I call radical purity!

Jesus called for radical purity, saying, "I tell you that anyone who looks at a woman lustfully has already committed adultery with her in his heart" (Matthew 5:28). Righteous Job said, "I made a covenant with my eyes not to look lustfully at a girl" (Job 31:1). I'm thankful that some men (women too) are making that commitment.

When I returned from three weeks in a Middle Eastern country, where women were very modestly dressed,[9] I was shocked when I arrived at the New York airport and saw glaring sexuality on every newsstand and on every television screen. My heart broke as I looked around at American women, many of them dressed as seductively as prostitutes. Ours has become an unholy culture.

I recently overheard a group of Christian men talking about how they have to discipline themselves to look the other way when they see a woman dressed seductively; otherwise they might stumble into mental adultery. I felt anger rising within me when I considered how difficult we as women often make it for men to remain mentally pure—just by the way we dress. I want to say to women—yes, even Christian women—"Have pity! Put some clothes on."

I'm convinced that the Holy Spirit is deeply grieved by many things in our culture that we take lightly. When he is grieved, he quietly walks away, and many of us don't even notice. While I am no advocate of legalism—I spent many years in an extremely legalistic church, so I have seen firsthand how it leads to either pride or rebellion—I believe we need to pursue a lifestyle of radical purity. Moment by moment we need to ask these questions of ourselves regarding any action we are taking:

- *Is what I am doing a choice for life?*
- *Is it helping me grow closer to God?*

- *Is it making it more—or less—likely that those streams of living water will continue flowing?*
- *Am I creating a stumbling block for others?*
- *Is it furthering my earnest desire to have power-packed faith?*
- *Is this choice I'm making right now the best use of my time?*
- *Is it the best image to view, the best thoughts to think, the best words to speak?*
- *Is it loving?*
- *Is it a reflection of my highest aspiration to love God and demonstrate his love to others?*

My pursuit of a lifestyle of radical purity has led me to the place where I don't watch television anymore, because it doesn't move me closer to becoming the woman I want to be. Neither do I listen to secular music, because I would much rather listen to uplifting messages. I don't watch R-rated films and am even cautious about PG-13 films. Purifying my lifestyle means I don't read women's magazines or secular novels, as I believe they fill my head with nonsense. I haven't got time for it!

Because I am committed to a lifestyle of purity, I'm not "a companion of fools" (Proverbs 13:20). I make outreach a lifestyle, and I love nonbelievers, but I don't spend so much time with them that they drag me down to their level. Instead, I seek to lift them up and point them to God. I don't engage in foolish talk, such as gossip, idle chatter about celebrities and television shows, or sexual innuendo and off-color jokes. Call me a prude or just flat-out rude, but if someone makes an inappropriate joke in front of me, I'll let it be known that it made me uncomfortable. (I'm learning to be a bit more tactful in my approach, so pray for me.) I try to quickly admit when I'm wrong—and I'm wrong a lot—and ask for forgiveness, whether I've offended my children, the bank teller, or the guy who just told a dirty joke in front of me.

Please understand. I am not trying to tell you what *you* need to do to purify your lifestyle. That is between you and God. These are the things God has led me to do so I can unleash his power in my life. He may ask different things of you. While I don't want to tell you what changes to make, I do want to challenge you to make some radical changes. It may mean unsubscribing to cable. It may mean getting Net Nanny to control the Web sites your family has access to. Pursuing a lifestyle of radical purity may even mean severing certain friendships, at least for a season.

Again, I want to reiterate that none of this is Christianity 101. None of these suggestions has anything to do with how much God loves you or whether he's going to let you into heaven. That's not what this book is about. This book is about becoming a vessel of God's power. If that's what you truly want, then you must purify your lifestyle, period. Purity is a prerequisite to unleashed power. "The friendship of the world is enmity with God" (James 4:4, KJV). You can have *friendship* with the world, or the power of God flowing through your life to *transform* the world. But you can't have both. Which do you choose?

―――⌐

Dear heavenly Father, thank you that I'm saved by grace, apart from anything I could ever do. Yet that same passage of Scripture reminds me that you've prepared good works you want me to perform. Lord, I know that the only truly good works that will be accomplished are those done through the power of the Holy Spirit at work in me. Thank you for bringing me to this place where experiencing your power at work in my life is more important than my current lifestyle. I am willing to make whatever lifestyle changes I need to make in order to be a more effective vessel for your glory. Show me, Holy Spirit, the specific changes I need to make…and help me not to go overboard by trying to turn those changes into laws! Amen.

AFFIRM

I choose a lifestyle of radical purity.

APPLY

1. What are some areas of your life where you tend toward impurity?

_____

_____

_____

2. Give an example of how that impure lifestyle might hinder God's power from flowing through your life.

_____

_____

_____

3. What was your reaction to the radical lifestyle changes the author was led to make? Do they seem extreme? reasonable?

_____

_____

_____

4. Describe your typical day. Consider which aspects of your lifestyle promote purity and which might be hindrances.

_____

_____

_____

5. What lifestyle changes is God calling you to make?

_____

_____

_____

𝒜CT

1. Take steps to implement the lifestyle changes God is laying on your heart.
2. Write out today's affirmation and scripture in your index-card notebook.
3. Write out your own prayer, expressing what God has shown you today about his mighty power.

_____

_____

_____

Meet Weekly
with Your PIT Crew

Two are better than one,
because they have a good return for their work:
If one falls down,
his friend can help him up.
But pity the man who falls
and has no one to help him up!

ECCLESIASTES 4:9–10

If you know anything about race-car driving, you know the purpose of a pit crew. It's a team of people who know exactly what they're doing and are committed to helping the driver finish the race successfully. The pit crew is highly skilled, efficient, and effective. It's not enough for the pit crew members to be sincere, because if they turn out to be sincerely wrong, the driver might crash. The same thing is true for us as Christians. God has called us to "run with perseverance the race marked out for us" (Hebrews 12:1). But we won't make it to the finish line without help. We need faith-boosting friends. That's why we all need what I call a PIT crew, which stands for:

- Prayer warriors
- Insightful counselors
- gifted Teachers

PRAYER WARRIORS

It's not enough for us to hunker down alone, fighting spiritual battles by ourselves. Frankly, it's easy to get weird when we go it alone. We need a group of people who pray with us and for us. Our experience of the power of God will, to a great extent, depend on the caliber of prayer warriors on our team. I know this from personal experience. I could tell you story after story of disastrous experiences I've had because I didn't have a strong team of prayer warriors supporting me. One particular example stands out in my mind. I made four cross-country trips and one international trip within a three-month period. My luggage was lost on all four of the domestic trips. *All four!* One woman suggested, "Maybe God is trying to tell you to stay home." Maybe she was right. But I believe the problems occurred because I didn't have prayer warriors praying for my protection as I traveled. You see, I had enough sense to galvanize prayer for my international trip, but I figured I could handle the domestic events with my own prayer efforts. Big, big, disastrous mistake. It's hard to be at your spiritual best when you're up all night trying to track down your luggage.

You don't have to be in full-time ministry to need a team of prayer warriors. Those who want to be vessels of God's power need to join forces with others who share that desire. So ask God to bring others into your life who will join you weekly to pray for opportunities to be part of seeing God's kingdom come and his will being done in your church, community, and the world.

INSIGHTFUL COUNSELORS

The Bible teaches that there is wisdom in the counsel of many: "Plans fail for lack of counsel, but with many advisers they succeed" (Proverbs 15:22). Again, we're on dangerous ground when we tell ourselves we have all the wisdom and can make all the right decisions without consulting others. There's nothing quite like a second opinion to provide us with a reality check! We all need a small group of people who will serve as our sounding board, people we've given permission to speak truth into our lives, because we respect them and know they have our best interests at heart.

I used to tell everyone I met about every problem in my life. My theme song was the spiritual that slaves in the South used to sing: "Nobody Knows the Trouble I've Seen." Since nobody knew the trouble I'd seen, I had to bring them up to date on all the latest. I figured maybe, just maybe, some stranger or casual acquaintance would have the right answer.

As you can tell, I was not only being foolish, I effectively *drove people away.* It's important not to consult with just anybody and everybody. Finding the right counselors takes great wisdom and much prayer. You will have a nervous breakdown if half the planet feels entitled to give you their opinion about how you should handle life's various predicaments. (Again, the voice of experience speaking here!) You'll be equally prone to a nervous breakdown if *no one* feels entitled to impart his or her wisdom to you. As always, the answer is balance. Ask God to bring wise people into your life, then grant them carte blanche to speak the truth as they see it.

GIFTED TEACHERS

I think my pastor is a fabulous Bible teacher. With at least thirty Lutheran pastors in his family lineage—including his father and grandfather—he ought to be! Fortunately for me, my pastor is not the only reason I appreciate my church. It has music that's just my speed, fabulous God-infused events, budget and program priorities I agree with, and much more. However, not everyone has the opportunity to attend a church where everything suits his or her fancy. Truth be told, few of us do.

During one season of my life, I had to choose between two churches: one had lots of great programs, enthusiastic participation in the worship service, and an active congregation filled with people who were in a similar stage of life as I was. It was within the same denomination as the church I had previously attended, so it was familiar to me in many ways. But for some reason, I almost never got a thing out of the weekly sermon. Although others loved the pastor's teaching, he didn't speak to me at all. Then I discovered a little Baptist church, filled with mostly older people. Stepping into the service was like stepping back in time, but when the preacher preached—oh my! His words went straight to my heart. Guess which church I attended? If you guessed the sleepy little Baptist church, you guessed correctly.

Before that, during my college years, even though the formal services at Tenth Presbyterian Church in downtown Philadelphia were not close to my personal preference, I often took a forty-five minute train ride on Sunday mornings to listen to Dr. James Montgomery Boice, one of the greatest Bible expositors of the modern era. During another season of life, I remained committed to my home church in the morning, but on Sunday evenings I often attended an Assemblies of God church to listen to the pastor, who had been raised in a Jewish home. He brought the Old Testament to life like few other preachers.

Now you know why I laugh when people try to peg me in a particular denominational box. I go wherever I find a good teacher. If we want to experience God's power, we are wise to open our eyes to what God is doing in a variety of churches all over the world. Sincere Christians have sincerely disagreed throughout church history. We can allow for sincere disagreement while preserving the unity of the body of Christ. One of the uppermost things on Jesus's mind was unity among his followers. Mutual love and respect among believers who believe differently is arguably the most compelling way we can demonstrate power-packed faith to a watching world, a world that is disgusted by the petty bickering that too often characterizes the church.

I realize, of course, that church selection is a personal matter that's well beyond the scope of this book. However, let me encourage you to have a *strong* Bible teacher in your life. If you love your church but do not get the teaching you need to build power-packed faith, attend a weekly Bible study led by a gifted teacher. I have on many occasions attended classes offered at churches that weren't my home church because it was the best available teaching. If you ever have the chance to attend Bible Study Fellowship, seize it. The teaching notes that accompany this program are among the best I've ever seen, and each group almost invariably has an outstanding lead teacher.[10]

Prayer warriors. Insightful counselors. Teachers who bring God's truth to life. There you have it: your very own PIT crew. Of course, your PIT crew won't do you any good if you never pull over and avail yourself of their skills. Why not make a regular appointment with your PIT crew? If you don't have a team assembled (most people don't—in fact, just writing this made me realize I have work to do), ask the Holy Spirit to show you whom to invite to be on board.

⌒

Dear heavenly Father, thank you so much for understanding my need to have many a "Jesus with skin on." Thank you for providing the body of Christ. Holy Spirit, lead me to the people I need who can

strengthen me for the race of life: prayer warriors, insightful counselors,
and gifted teachers. Help me to open my heart and be willing to
learn and benefit from the strengths of others. At the same time,
I want to be part of the PIT crew for other believers. Show me
practical ways I can become a more effective prayer warrior, counselor,
and, within my own sphere, a capable teacher of your truth. Amen.

AFFIRM

I need a PIT crew: prayer warriors, insightful counselors, and gifted teachers.

APPLY

1. Who are the prayer warriors in your life? How often do you gather with them? Do you need to make arrangements to assemble an effective prayer team?

_____

_____

_____

2. Who are the insightful counselors in your life? Do you seek their wisdom before making important life decisions?

_____

_____

_____

3. Do you have an outstanding Bible teacher in your life? Do you need to find a weekly Bible study led by a strong teacher?

_____

_____

_____

4. Describe the ideal operation of your PIT crew. How would you like to see it functioning in your life?

_____

_____

_____

5. Who will you contact about being part of your PIT crew? Do you need to volunteer to be part of someone else's PIT crew? (Ideally, there is crossover between the two.)

_____

_____

_____

ACT

1. Enlist your PIT crew. Begin by contacting prayer warriors. If you do not know any, attend your church's next weekly prayer meeting, and you'll likely meet a few. One hint: look to the gray-haired crowd. Next, ask your pastor to recommend some insightful counselors, and again, be alert to the senior saints who have amassed years of wisdom that they'd probably love to share with you. Finally, you need great teachers. Find out about the classes offered in your church and community.

2. Write out today's affirmation and scripture in your index-card notebook.

3. Write out your own prayer, expressing what God has shown you today about his mighty power.

_____

_____

_____

_____

Abandon Clock-Controlled and Checklist-Driven Bible Reading

I seek you with all my heart;
do not let me stray from your
commands.
I have hidden your word in my heart
that I might not sin against you.
Praise be to you, O LORD;
teach me your decrees.
With my lips I recount
all the laws that come from your
mouth.
I rejoice in following your statutes
as one rejoices in great riches.
I meditate on your precepts
and consider your ways.
I delight in your decrees;
I will not neglect your word.

PSALM 119:10–16

*D*id you know it's possible to read the Bible and get *absolutely nothing* out of it? When Bible reading doesn't convict and inspire us, it can do more harm than good.

You're in shock. You can't believe a Bible teacher just made such statements. But let me explain. Stalin not only read the Bible; it's said he memorized the entire New Testament. Joseph Smith, founder of Mormonism, not only read the Bible; he obviously knew it well enough to plagiarize vast portions of it in *The Book of Mormon*. The religion professor at my university not only read the Bible; he taught the Bible—as an intriguing piece of antiquity and a quaint collection of fairy tales. These people read the Bible, but they didn't allow it to change their hearts and lives. As a result, they'll be judged by a tougher standard when they stand before God.

Satan is another example of someone who used his knowledge of the Bible for evil rather than good. Think about it. He had to have known the Bible, or how else was he able to quote it to Jesus? (see Matthew 4:1–11). How else is he so effective in twisting it in people's minds, whether to deceive Christians or create cults and false religions? Satan is the "father of lies" (John 8:44), and you can be sure he is behind all such distortions. James indicates that all demons have great doctrine: "You believe that there is one God. Good! Even the demons believe that—and shudder" (2:19). So Bible reading and sound doctrine can inform us, but they don't automatically transform us.

God's Word holds no power to transform our lives apart from the Spirit of God illuminating it. It's nothing more than marks on a page. Unless we approach God's Word with a teachable spirit, it will *not* penetrate, and it will not judge our thoughts and attitudes (see Hebrews 4:12). As Christians, we often fail to benefit from Bible reading because we approach God's Word in the wrong spirit or for the wrong reasons. Maybe we are reading out of duty so we can congratulate ourselves as we check that item off our daily to-do list. (That was me!) Perhaps we have the heart of a know-it-all and only read the Bible to show off our knowledge or to prove everyone else wrong. (Yep, another of my personal specialties!)

If we read the Bible thinking, *Well, I can set so-and-so straight with this verse,* or, *This sure disproves that theology,* we are not being teachable—so the Teacher steps out of the room. I've found that God uses his Word to convict me and encourage others; not vice versa. He doesn't say, *Donna, you've arrived, but Shelly could sure use a talkin' to!* Reading the Bible does encourage me, but never to stay the way I am.

If we want to be vessels of God's power, reading his Word must become more than a duty or informative religious exercise. Now, that doesn't mean we should have goose bumps or hear the "Hallelujah" chorus every time we pick up the Bible, but it *is* a living book. What do I mean by living? Well, how can you tell when a person is alive? They *communicate* with you. Even when someone is in a coma, doctors urge people to keep lines of communication open, with the hope that it will bring the person back to consciousness. (Isn't it interesting that people even try to communicate with the dead to keep their friends and loved ones "alive" to them?) As a living book, the Bible communicates with us. It speaks to our circumstances; it gives us just the answer we need, when we need it. That's why we should ask specific questions when we read the Bible and expect the Holy Spirit to provide clear, unmistakable answers. We should perceive that he is customizing the curriculum, showing us which of *our own* thoughts and attitudes need to change.

As we read God's Word, the Holy Spirit brings it to life for us. One of the most vivid examples I can recall from my own life occurred in Papua New Guinea, an island nation where, as recently as the 1960s, headhunters and cannibals roamed. Even today, isolated tribes speak more than seven hundred different languages. Sitting in my small cabin in the middle of the jungle, I was suddenly gripped with overwhelming insecurity and anxiety. What could I possibly say to these people living in a world so different from my own? Everything within me wanted to run to the nearest airport and hightail it back to the United States.

I picked up my Bible and asked God, *What on earth am I doing here? Is this all a big mistake?* The Holy Spirit led me to Isaiah 49:1–3:

Listen to me, you islands;
    hear this, you distant nations:
Before I was born the LORD called me;
    from my birth he has made mention of my name.

He made my mouth like a sharpened sword,
    in the shadow of his hand he hid me;
he made me into a polished arrow
    and concealed me in his quiver.

He said to me, "You are my servant,
    Israel, in whom I will display my splendor."

As those words leaped off the page at me, I knew God was reassuring me that I really was his servant, that he had indeed called me to minister to the people of Papua New Guinea, and that he would display his splendor in spite of my inadequacies. I had asked a question, and through his living Word, God had joined the conversation with a clear, unmistakable answer.

Is the Bible alive to you? Have you experienced the power of God through his life-giving Word? If not, you are missing out on a blessing. Simply invite the Holy Spirit to be who he is: your Teacher. Remember, Jesus said he was sending him to guide us into *all* truth (see John 16:13).

Apart from him, we are ever open to lies and half truths. Open your heart to his instruction.

If we want to experience God's power, we can't ignore God's Word or dabble in it. We must be like the psalmist—we must saturate ourselves in it. It takes time to know God's Word. Not rushed time. Leisurely time. As much time as it takes to hear God's voice. Ezra read aloud from the Book of the Law of Moses "from daybreak till noon," and "all the people listened attentively," *standing while he read* (see Nehemiah 8:1–6). We expect to receive a gold star if we read the Bible for fifteen minutes, snuggled up in our comfy bed!

If the clock or a checklist governs our approach to Bible reading, it's unlikely that we'll experience the fullness of power available through God's Word. There's a heart issue here. When we say to the Holy Spirit, *You've got five minutes—or five chapters—to teach me something,* I believe we are insulting him. The Bible says it's possible to both "grieve" and "quench" the Holy Spirit (Ephesians 4:30; 1 Thessalonians 5:19, AMP). Clock-controlled and checklist-driven Bible reading can cause both.

Instead, our attitude should be: *You're the Teacher, and I believe you have much to teach me; I have much to learn. I have thoughts and attitudes that need to change. Search me. Try me. I'm here, sitting at your feet, and I'll remain here until you tell me the lesson is over.*

Right about now you're thinking: *This woman is crazy! She doesn't know the first thing about my hectic schedule. I haven't got time to sit around reading the Bible. The minute I get out of bed, I have to leap into action. And I'm on the run all day until I finally collapse into bed at night. When am I supposed to enjoy all this leisurely Bible reading?*

We deceive ourselves into thinking we have to do things that aren't our jobs—my family *needs* me; my boss *needs* me; my friends *need* me. While we have certain obligations and responsibilities that God wants us to fulfill, we often try to do it *all*…to take care of *everything*. Ironically, we often try to do these things on our own, apart from God. What better time to unleash the power of God than when it feels as though we don't have time to get everything done we need to do? Don't we need the power of God more than ever during such times? It is madness to think that we have anything more powerful to offer than the power of God.

Think about it. God is the provider. God is the all-sufficient one. God is the counselor. When his power flows through us, we can be who we need to be for our friends and families. The most important thing we can give our children is not more toys or more trips to Disneyland. It's the privilege of being raised by a God-saturated parent—one who prays before speaking, one who extends grace and forgiveness, one who constantly includes God in decision making, one who invites God into all aspects of life and applies wisdom from his Word to every situation. The most valuable thing we can offer an employer is to be a God-infused employee—one who walks in peace, speaks wisdom, and operates with integrity. Nothing we can offer *apart from God* can have more positive impact on the world than what God can do *through us* as we allow him to first work *in us*.

We need to make it a daily priority to sit at the feet of Jesus. We need to take time in God's Word so it can transform us from the inside out, thus unleashing his power to flow through us. When we do, our work is more effective. We can speak one God-infused sentence or take one action prompted by the Holy Spirit, and transform someone's life. While leisurely time in the Word may not seem like an efficient approach to the Christian life, it is the only *effective* approach.

When you put yourself under the Holy Spirit's tutelage, he's not going to say, *Aha! Just what I've been waiting for! Now I can shipwreck her life by destroying her schedule and preventing her from getting anything accomplished. This is my big chance to make her family and co-workers furious with her by making her neglect her responsibilities.* Quite the opposite. He will be so overjoyed, he will go out of his way to ensure your efficiency. He will enable you to get more done in less time and with far less aggravation. He may even prove to you that when you stop being everyone's rescuer, people suddenly step up to the plate and become more responsible.

No one *has* the time to devote to God's Word. No one ever *finds* the time. But there are those who have chosen to *make* the time. It's a simple matter of priorities, because when the day is done, we have all chosen to do whatever we have chosen to do. As always, life is a matter of choices. We can cling to efficiency, approaching Bible reading as a task to be accomplished. Or we can open our hearts to a new and better way, granting the Holy Spirit as much time as he needs to transform us into effective conduits of the power of God. Efficient or effective. It's up to us.

~~~~~

Dear heavenly Father, at times I've preferred efficiency over effectiveness. I've told myself I have more important things to do than sit still, allowing the Holy Spirit to teach me from your Word. My approach has been shortsighted. What I really want is effectiveness. I want to become an agent of your grace. Holy Spirit, forgive me for grieving you with my checklists and charts. Forgive me for quenching your work in my life. You are the Teacher, and you know what I need to learn and how long it will take to learn those lessons. I open my heart to you. I know I'll never have the time or find the time, but I'm making a decision in this moment: I will, with your enabling grace, make the time to humble myself and learn from you. Amen.

AFFIRM

There's no substitute for time spent in God's Word.

APPLY

1. How much time do you spend reading God's Word? Is your time in God's Word clock controlled or checklist driven? How so?

   _____

   _____

   _____

2. Do you suspect that your clock-controlled or checklist-driven approach has hindered the Holy Spirit from teaching you the lessons he had in mind? Explain your answer.

   _____

   _____

   _____

3. Recall a time when God spoke to you very specifically from his Word. Describe the circumstance and the impact of what God told you.

_____

_____

_____

4. Describe a time when you read God's Word in a leisurely way, giving the Holy Spirit as much time as he needed to teach you the lesson he had in mind.

_____

_____

_____

5. Practically speaking, what changes do you need to make to shift from an efficient approach to Scripture reading...to an effective approach to life?

_____

_____

_____

ACT

1. Pick up your Bible and read until the Holy Spirit teaches you something specific and personal *for your life*. Ask him to reveal something to you about your thoughts, attitudes, or circumstances.

2. Write out today's affirmation and scripture in your index-card notebook.

3. Write out your own prayer, expressing what God has shown you today about his mighty power.

_____

_____

_____

_____

Highlight God's Word

Your word is a lamp to my feet
and a light for my path.

PSALM 119:105

I hadn't color-coded my Bible in more than a decade. That was when my first Bible, with more verses highlighted than not, fell apart from overuse. Since then, no Bible has become my single customized companion. Instead, I started a Bible collection. You name it, I have it on my shelf: Life Application Bible, Serendipity Small Group Bible, Narrated Bible, One-Year Bible, Leadership Bible, The Message, The Amplified Bible, and a slim-line edition that I can't even read, and my trusty online Bible, which is the one I use most often. In addition, I bought what I have dubbed my travel Bible.

My travel Bible is that rarest of rarities these days: an ordinary Bible. It's not a BBQ-Lovers Bible or a Mothers of Teenage Girls Bible. It's just…a Bible. No comments. No elaborate charts or sidebars. No fancy structure. No special margins. A Bible. Plain and profound.

A couple of months ago, I was overcome with an irresistible urge to buy colored pencils in the first of several airports I was to visit that day. That's when I rediscovered the joy of coloring. The flights flew by as I colored and colored. I even found the layovers surprisingly enjoyable, as I sat engrossed by my color-coding project.

Obviously, I wasn't coloring for coloring's sake. Any serious student will tell you that highlighting important points in the course textbook is fundamental to learning, not to mention preparing for and passing tests. Not that the Bible is a mere textbook, but as students in the school of life, instructed by the Holy Spirit, we should approach our study of God's Word with equal vigor.

So, as I held that brand-new box of pencils in my hand, I prayed, *Where should I begin?* The answer I received was: *Prayer.* The obvious place to start was with Jesus's model prayer, which he taught the disciples when they asked him how to pray. I turned to Matthew 6:9–15 and meditated on the prayer as I colored it blue (just because it was the prettiest color in the box!). From there, the Holy Spirit prompted me to search out and highlight the parable of the persistent widow (see Luke 18:1–8) and Jesus's final prayers for himself, his disciples, and all believers (see John 17). God used these passages to show me that prayer is not a magic wand to solve all our problems; sometimes it's a tool to strengthen us to endure trials. Sometimes prayer unleashes God's power to deliver us from difficult situations; other times it unleashes the power for us to make it through.

Next, I did something I'd never done before: I turned to the mini-concordance in the back of my travel Bible and highlighted every reference it listed on prayer, meditating as I colored and asking God to teach me something from each one. "This is so cool," I said aloud, as the guy next to me raised his eyebrows at a forty-something woman coloring with glee.

From prayer, I moved on to peace. Since I am a recovering adrenaline junkie and certified drama queen, the Holy Spirit never tires of teaching me about my ever great need to "seek peace and pursue it" (Psalm 34:14). As I colored and meditated on peace passages, I noticed how often peace was tied to right living. For example, the Bible says: "righteousness and peace kiss each other" (Psalm 85:10); "Discipline your son, and he will give you peace" (Proverbs 29:17). Having worn down my peaceful-looking, pink-colored pencil, I turned my attention to passages on wisdom, which I marked with a purple crown. Not surprisingly, the book of Proverbs in my Bible is now covered with purple crowns (see Proverbs 1:1–7, 20; 2:1–22; 3:13–26; 4:5–11; 5:1; 9:10–12; 10:13–14; 18:15; 19:11; 24:3–7, to name just a few).

As I studied wisdom, I marveled at how often it's linked to right pathways. For example, "Listen, my son, and be wise, and keep your heart on the right path" (Proverbs 23:19). So I marked the verses about pathways green and sometimes even drew a squiggly green road in the margin. Then I noticed that wisdom and prosperity are often linked, and I began marking references to prosperity, business, and financial management with green dollar signs.

This past Sunday morning at church, during the announcements (when I would normally doodle on the bulletin), I grabbed an orange pencil and started highlighting every mention I could find of the word *hope*. I had been feeling incredibly hopeless lately, and this exercise lifted my spirits and boosted my faith. I was especially encouraged with this prayer, "May the God of hope fill you with all joy and peace as you trust in him, so that you may overflow with hope by the power of the Holy Spirit" (Romans 15:13). As I said, color-coding your Bible is not coloring for coloring's sake. It's a tool for studying, meditating, and making connections among passages. It's for noticing trends, contrasts, similarities, lists, and so on. Customizing your Bible is just another way of sharpening your sword. It's about cooperating with the Holy Spirit as he leads you to highlight those verses that he wants to use in your life to instruct and change you.

Just last Saturday, the Holy Spirit led me to spend two hours highlighting every occurrence I could find of God calling an individual. In Genesis, the Lord calls Abram, speaks clearly to him, gives him a specific assignment, and tells him what would happen in his future (see Genesis 15). In the last book of the Bible, Revelation, God calls upon John to testify about what is to come. I saw God calling individuals from Genesis to Revelation. God calls us and cares about our future.

In some instances, God's call is explicit, as when he appeared to Moses at the burning bush (see Exodus 3:1–22) and told him to deliver the Israelites from the hand of Pharaoh, or when he called Jeremiah to be a prophet to the nations (see Jeremiah 1:4–19). In other cases, God's call is implicit in the situation. For example, Nehemiah did not hear directly from God. Instead, he heard from his brother about the "great trouble and disgrace" in Jerusalem (see Nehemiah 1:2–3). The call was implied, not stated. The same was true for Esther. Her cousin Mordecai, not God, told her, "If you remain silent at this time, relief and deliverance for the Jews will arise from another place, but you and your father's family will perish. And who knows but that you have come to royal position for such a time as this?" (Esther 4:14).

Both Nehemiah and Esther answered God's call, and became vessels of his power. Nehemiah fulfilled his call by rebuilding the walls of Jerusalem in fifty-two days, and Esther fulfilled hers by saving the Jewish people from genocide. I plan to continue studying these passages so I can learn everything they reveal about how God calls and commissions his people for service. Then I can use what I learn to teach others, challenging them to step out and fulfill the call of God on their lives, whether that call is explicit or implicit.

When we mark verses that the Holy Spirit uses to unleash God's power in our lives, we will find it easier to teach others as God unleashes his power and works through us. For instance, the Bible says God comforts us so that we'll be able to comfort others. It's reasonable to expect God to bring people into your life who are facing the same types of trials you've lived through. Let's say you've lost a child and the Holy Spirit teaches you about grief recovery. If you marked the verses that ministered most effectively to you, then when God brings a grieving parent across your path, you can easily find those passages, and the Holy Spirit can bring to your mind truths that will bring healing to that grieving person.

When I recently lost a friend, God brought me back to a passage he gave me when I lost a child several years ago. In 2 Samuel 12, we read that David's son (with Bathsheba) was gravely ill. David fasted and prayed, pleading with God to heal his child and refusing to get up from the ground. However, when the child died, David immediately got up, got dressed, went into the house of the Lord to worship, then went home and ate. His servants were stunned. They couldn't understand why he was acting this way, assuming he would be far worse once the baby was dead and all hope was lost.

But David explained, "While the child was still alive, I fasted and wept. I thought, 'Who knows? The LORD may be gracious to me and let the child live.' But now that he is dead, why should I fast? Can I bring him back again? I will go to him, but he will not return to me" (2 Samuel 12:22–23). These verses hold a promise of heaven—a promise that we'll see our loved ones again. It also answers the age-old question, "Will we see our babies in heaven if they died before coming to personal faith?" This passage tells us we will. I have two children waiting there for me, so this promise is especially precious to me.

I spoke on this passage at my friend's funeral, and many people approached me afterward to say it was exactly what they needed to hear; I told them I only shared what God had given me.

Are you ready to sharpen your sword so God can unleash his power in your life? Ask your personal tutor, the Holy Spirit, which subject you should study. If you don't hear a clear answer, assume he wants to strengthen areas of weakness in your life. No doubt you know what those are. For example, if you struggle with your tongue, color the following verses red as you meditate on them: Psalm 39:1; Proverbs 12:18; James 1:26; 3:8. If finances are a challenge, study and color green: Proverbs 24:30–34; 27:23–27; 28:19–20; Matthew 25:14–30.

God only knows what adventure he has in store for you as you become an eager student in the Holy Spirit's Bible School. Have your colored pencils ready!

Note: My former pastor's wife, a spiritual giant if ever I've known one, never makes any marks in her Bible. She prefers to have a fresh encounter with God's Word without any preconceived ideas about a particular passage from previous lessons. I respect her decision; it's okay if you feel the same way.

⟡

Dear heavenly Father, I stand in awe of the infinitely creative ways you've provided for us to learn from you. Thank you for the many Bible choices available to Christians today. I want to take this moment to pray for those believers who do not yet have a complete Bible in their own language; I pray you would strengthen

Bible translators and send new workers for the many languages still without the Bible. I thank you for my Bible. Help me to appreciate it for the powerful spiritual weapon it truly is. Holy Spirit, teach me how to use my Bible as effectively as possible. Amen.

AFFIRM

When I customize my Bible, I am sharpening my sword.

APPLY

1. If your Bible were lost, how lost would you be? How personal, and therefore irreplaceable, is it?

   _____

   _____

   _____

2. What do you think of the suggestion to color-code your Bible? What do you see as the advantages (and perhaps even disadvantages)?

_____

_____

_____

3. What are some other ways you might customize your Bible?

_____

_____

_____

4. Describe a time when you were excited about Bible study. What sparked your enthusiasm, and how can you recover that spark, if it seems to be fading?

_____

_____

_____

5. What are some key topics you might begin highlighting—and studying?

_____

_____

_____

ACT

1. Begin customizing your Bible in fresh, new ways. Try to invest at least thirty minutes in this starting exercise.

2. Write out today's affirmation and scripture in your index-card notebook.

3. Write out your own prayer, expressing what God has shown you today about his mighty power.

_____

_____

_____

_____

Take God's Word Personally

Your statutes are my heritage forever;
they are the joy of my heart.

PSALM 119:III

I first learned the importance of making God's Word personal when my friend Amy put her finger on my fundamental problem. She said, "Donna, you believe the Bible in theory, but you don't seem to believe it's true *for you* in practical ways. It's almost like you think God so loved the world, except for Donna. You believe Jesus came that people might have life and live it to the full. That's great for 'people,' but what about *you*? You don't have faith; all you have is good doctrine!"

Although stunned by her comments—and maybe even insulted—I couldn't deny that Amy routinely experienced the power of God in ways that had eluded me. An unshakable joy and healthy God-confidence permeated her life and touched those she encountered. She knew her faults but didn't hate herself. In fact, Amy didn't waste much time thinking about herself one way or the other. She kept her focus on loving God and helping others. When Amy showed up, God's power showed up too. When she prayed, *something happened*!

I wanted to experience power-packed faith in my life in the way that Amy did. I wanted the Holy Spirit to shape me and change me in practical and tangible ways so I would be a conduit of God's power. I decided to learn Amy's secret. She told me that God had transformed her life as she began to make the Bible personal. "My faith was powerless," she said. "I claimed to believe all the right things, but my faith wasn't *working*. When I read the Bible, I felt worse about myself. All I saw was how I wasn't measuring up. But picking myself apart didn't make me a better person; in fact, I felt so badly about myself that I picked everybody *else* apart too. I wanted to bring them down to my level. Even though I believed all the right things and was in full-time ministry, I was a miserable Christian. Something was wrong."

Amy resigned from the ministry and sat down in her small apartment, all alone, crying out to God. Weeks went by, with Amy just sitting there, determined to hear from God. Everyone wondered what on earth she was thinking. Then one day she sensed God saying, *You need a revelation of my love. You need to see yourself as I see you.*

Amy says, "Just then, I felt the love of God begin flowing over me. It's hard to describe. Wave after wave washed over me, sweeping away all the self-hate and insecurities. I knew God loved me. And only a constant awareness of his great love for me would enable me to love others. You can't give others what you don't have yourself."

Amy's next step was learning to see herself as God sees her. "The only identity my theology had imparted to me was, 'I am a wretched sinner.' I viewed everyone else as wretched sinners too, even my fellow Christians. No wonder I felt lousy about myself and had a lousy attitude toward everyone I met. God showed me, through his Word, that my view was distorted. The Holy Spirit led me to search out every Scripture passage that spoke to my identity in Christ. He prompted me to take out a notebook and rewrite every passage, making it personal. For example, 'You did not choose me, but I chose you…to go and bear fruit,' became, 'God chose *me*! God handpicked me to go bear fruit.' 'We are God's workmanship, created in Christ Jesus to do good works,' became, '*I* am God's workmanship. *I've* been created to do good works.' On and on it went. Page after page, filled with positive, personal statements of Scripture, such as, *I am hidden with Christ in God. The devil can't even find me. I am the salt of the earth. I am God's temple. I am a saint. I am chosen and dearly loved.*

Eventually, Amy had more than four hundred positive, personalized scriptures she regularly recited aloud, over and over. For more than six months, she spent anywhere from two to ten hours a day, basking in God's love, praising him, and reciting the personalized passages. She then recorded them and played the tape over and over again, even while she slept.

Today Amy is back in full-time ministry, traveling the world as a powerful Bible teacher and evangelist. She spends most of her time among unreached people groups in Muslim and Buddhist nations. She goes where no one else will go and boldly proclaims the gospel in the power of God. She still devotes at least an hour each day to reciting her positive, personalized scriptures aloud. She says it is the key to unleashing the power of God in her life.

At Amy's urging, I started praying that the Holy Spirit would make the Bible become personal to me, and I began personalizing the scriptures on her list (which she graciously e-mailed to me). I gradually customized the list with additional scriptures the Holy Spirit led me to include. Following Amy's example, I sat in my prayer room for at least an hour each day, reciting the verses aloud. Some of my personalized scriptures include:

- The Enemy may come against me one way, but he'll be forced to flee from me seven ways! (see Deuteronomy 28:7).
- No weapon that's formed against me will prosper. All those who rise up against me will fall. Every accusation made against me will be refuted (see Isaiah 54:17).

- I know today will be a great day, because God's mercies are new every morning (see Lamentations 3:23).
- Today I will know firsthand the love of Christ, which passes knowledge, and I will be filled with the fullness of God (see Ephesians 3:19).
- I'm not going to be afraid of anything today, because God has not given me a spirit of fear but of love, power, and a sound mind (see 2 Timothy 1:7).

All of the verses the Holy Spirit showed me address major problems in my personality. I am pessimistic, so it helps me to greet each day with a positive attitude (see Lamentations 3:23). Because I'm in public ministry, I have my share of accusatory critics. The Isaiah 54:17 passage tells me no attack can succeed as long as I'm doing what God has called me to do. Even if the attack is satanic, God is big enough to handle it (see Deuteronomy 28:7). I struggle with fear and insecurity, so reminding myself of God's love helps me overcome my fears (see Ephesians 3:19 and 2 Timothy 1:7).

When I began reciting personalized scriptures, my friends noticed a dramatic change in me within six months. They said I seemed more secure, peaceful, and God-confident. Some even said I looked younger! This, in turn, has made me a more effective vessel of God's power. Personalized, positive scriptures have empowered my walk with God unlike anything else I've ever experienced.

For your convenience, I've included a preliminary list of personalized verses starting on page 257 this book. However, let the Holy Spirit be your Teacher. He can do much better than I can, because he knows your areas of greatest need. Why not ask him to help you create your own list of verses to personalize? When you are color-coding your Bible, ask him to alert you to verses you can personalize and add to your list for recitation. God's Word is packed with power; making it personal makes it even more powerful.

Dear heavenly Father, thank you for your powerful Word. Thank you for reminding me that you have wonderful things to say about me. Yes, I still sin, but I am no longer a "wretched sinner," thanks to Jesus. Holy Spirit, please lead me into all truth, and help me not to cling to lies or half truths. Flood me with a revelation of God's great love for me, so I can demonstrate that love to others. Guide me as I create a list of personalized verses that speak to my areas of greatest need. I want to experience the power of God through his Word, transforming me and enabling me to impact the world for Jesus. Amen.

Affirm

God's Word has the power to transform me, especially when I make it personal.

Apply

1. Do you think God is disappointed with you? that you aren't measuring up? Or are you profoundly aware that you are dearly loved? Explain your answer.

_____

_____

_____

2. What is your current identity? Is it in alignment with who God
   says you are? If you aren't sure who God says you are or what he
   thinks of you, turn to "Personalized Scriptures" (page 257).
   Then note your response below.

_____

_____

_____

3. Have you ever been overwhelmed with the realization of God's
   great love for you? Have you ever experienced a moment when
   wave upon wave of his love washed over you? If so, describe
   below. If not, ask God to give you such an experience, then note
   your reaction.

_____

_____

_____

4. What was your reaction to Amy's decision to spend hours each
   day reciting Scripture aloud?

_____

_____

_____

5. On the lines below, write out some of your own personalized scriptures. You can also begin adding these to your index-card notebook.

_____

_____

_____

𝒜ct

1. Begin your list of personalized scriptures. Consider recording your list and listening to it, over and over again—maybe even while you're sleeping!
2. Write out today's affirmation and scripture in your index-card notebook.
3. Write out your own prayer, expressing what God has shown you today about his mighty power.

_____

_____

_____

_____

Let God Unleash the Power of His Word Through You

The word of God is living and active. Sharper than any double-edged sword, it penetrates even to dividing soul and spirit, joints and marrow; it judges the thoughts and attitudes of the heart.

HEBREWS 4:12

God's Word is living and active, sharper than any two-edged sword. It cuts right to the heart of the matter. Not only can the Holy Spirit use it to transform us from the inside out, as discussed yesterday, he can also unleash the power of God's Word through us, as a surgical tool in the spiritual lives of those around us.

On the Day of Pentecost, Peter stood before a gathered crowd, quoting extensively from the book of Joel and the psalms of David. Declaring, among other things, that "everyone who calls on the name of the Lord will be saved" (Acts 2:21). The Bible tells us, "When the people heard this, they were cut to the heart and said to Peter and the other apostles, 'Brothers, what shall we do?'" (Acts 2:37). God's Word, spoken through the mouth of a believer, led three thousand people to salvation that day.

God's Word remains just as powerful today. The following story illustrates that power, but I need to clarify that this is *not* an example of how wonderful and superspiritual I am. I give it as evidence of how awesome and powerful *God* is and how eager he is to work through *anyone* who is willing to be willing. What God did through me, he wants to do through *you.*

Let me set the stage. Susie Shellenberger of Focus on the Family had just delivered a powerful message to an audience of six hundred people, most of them teens or college students. She instructed us to gather into our preassigned teams of thirty to forty and pray over each young person on our team, asking God to show each one what was blocking his work in his or her life. The Holy Spirit prompted me to grab my Bible as the first young girl climbed onto the mat for prayer.

As she poured out her heart, he led me to a verse that spoke directly to this girl's situation. She was grappling with repeated temptations to suicide; God led me to read to her Deuteronomy 30:11–20, which instructs us how to live and tells us to, "Choose life." Then a young man who was facing challenges with his classmates climbed onto the mat. Again, the Holy Spirit prompted me to read Scripture over him, promising him that he would be as Joshua: "No one will be able to stand up against you all the days of your life" (Joshua 1:5). Over and over again, God led me to just the right passage. I felt a mixture of awe and fear. Awe at how precisely the passages spoke to each person's circumstance, but fear that I wouldn't have a verse to give the next person. There were almost forty people gathered around that prayer mat. As the fear and insecurity began welling up in me, I sensed God was almost chuckling at my foolishness and saying, *You're not* finding *verses, Donna. I'm* handing *them to you. This isn't about you or your ability to find the right verse. It's about your availability and willingness to read the passages I'm giving you.* Instantly, the insecurity left, and

I knew that even if all forty people asked for prayer, God would lead me to forty passages of Scripture. God was faithful right down to the last person who wanted encouragement.

Afterward, I talked with some of the young people to determine if these passages were indeed right on target. A young woman who had received a passage challenging her to "walk before [the Lord] and be blameless" (Genesis 17:1) told me that many of her closest friends had recently started drinking; she knew God was telling her she needed to find new friends. She has e-mailed me since returning to school and has continued strong in her faith. She has even undertaken her own private study of everything the Bible teaches about being blameless. God spoke to another young girl about ministry to native peoples, and he later confirmed this by leading her, during an outdoor devotional time, to a lone cactus plant in the middle of jungle foliage.

Another young woman said she was so excited about the message God had given her, she had immediately called her parents and told them God had spoken to her from Isaiah 40:1, "Comfort, comfort my people," indicating that her primary life mission was comforting Christians. Her parents confirmed that this was the ministry they also believed God had in mind for her, and they promised to support her as she prepared for that role. I have also heard several times from the girl with suicidal tendencies, and, thank God, she is choosing life. God's Word *is* power packed!

After our prayer time, I returned to my room and sat looking at my Bible for a long, long time. I thought of all the wonderful Christian books I had read, all the wonderful sermons I had heard, all the songs that had blessed my soul, and all the audio tapes and video-teaching series I had enjoyed. I realized they were all well and good, as long as they pointed me to God. However, God hadn't used any of those things to work through me that night. Instead, the Holy Spirit worked through God's Word alone.

That night something inside me changed. While I will continue reading Christian books, listening to sermons, and attending conferences, I realized they had become *too high a priority* in my life. Too often, given a choice between reading my Bible or reading a Christian book, I chose the book. Too often, I've substituted time spent listening to audio tapes for time spent reading the Bible. God has shown me that his Word *must* be first.

George Müller, a mighty man of faith who operated orphanages in England during the nineteenth century, went so far as to give away every book he owned—except the Bible. Yes, he even got rid of his Bible commentaries and collection of Christian books. He owned one book only: the Bible. I'm not planning to go to that extreme, but I do pray I'll never again lose sight of the real power source.

Judy Lovitt recounts an experience of God's Spirit using God's Word through her to help someone else. A woman in her church, Fay, approached her one Sunday and said, "I know you are a woman of the Word. Would you please pray and ask God if he has a verse for me?" Judy thought the request was unusual, but since she respected Fay, she was open to the idea. She recalls, "I went home and sat down with a blank notebook, pen, and my Bible. I asked God to show me something for Fay. Then I sat and wrote what came to my mind. I ended up with some thoughts and three pages of verses about battle." Again, Judy was caught off guard, because she didn't perceive Fay as being swept up into any sort of battle.

However, three weeks later, she gave the handwritten notes to Fay, who said the verses addressed, point by point, the exact issues she was facing. Judy was almost more astonished than Fay, as she never would have volunteered for such an assignment. "The Holy Spirit truly did give me the right verses for Fay," Judy recalls. "We were both excited and practically jumping up and down. I recently talked with her, and she is still excited about how well the verses fit her need at the moment."

Just to be certain we stay in balance, let me share a postscript to my story about the night of praying "on the mat." One young woman didn't request prayer that evening, yet I felt the Lord saying, *She needs to know there's "a door of hope."* I recognized the phrase from Scripture but wasn't sure where it was found. However, since the girl didn't step forward, I didn't think anymore about it. A month later, she e-mailed me to say she had finally stepped on the prayer mat, all alone before God, and he had instructed her—loudly and clearly—to turn to Hosea 2:14–15: "Therefore I am now going to allure her; I will lead her into the desert and speak tenderly to her. There I will give her back her vineyards, and will make the Valley of Achor a door of hope." *I never mentioned that passage of Scripture to this girl or anyone else.* The Holy Spirit gave it directly to her.

Clearly, God doesn't *need* us. He can always bypass us entirely, cut right through the middleman, and speak directly to his children. But if we want to become vessels of God's power, we must be willing for him to use us. When it comes to experiencing God's power, we don't *have to.* We *get to.*

Right now, I'm busy sharpening my sword, praying with expectation for the next time the Holy Spirit will give me the unspeakable privilege of wielding it.

~~~~~

*Dear heavenly Father, I marvel at the power of your Word.
I acknowledge that there is no other book, no audio tape, no video
series, no resource, no matter how wonderful, that can compare with
the power of your Word. Holy Spirit, I want to become an avid
student of the Bible. I look forward to all the wonderful truths and
practical lessons you have in store for me. Thank you for extending
to me the incredible privilege of wielding the Word. Amen.*

$\mathcal{A}$FFIRM

God's power is unleashed through me as I share his Word with others.

$\mathcal{A}$PPLY

1. Recall a time when someone gave you "just the right scripture." Describe the message and the impact it had on your life.

   _____

   _____

   _____

2. Recall a time when you knew God used you to give someone else "just the right scripture." Describe the impact. If you are still in touch with that person, call her and ask about the long-term effects of that Word in her life.

   _____

   _____

   _____

3. What did you think of George Müller's decision to give away every book other than his Bible?

_____

_____

_____

4. Do you tend to spend more time reading Christian books, listening to tapes, and so on, than you do studying God's Word? Why do you think that is? Do you feel the need to make any changes?

_____

_____

_____

5. Can you think of someone, right now, who needs a message from God's Word? Pray, asking God to lead you to a scripture that will speak directly to the situation. Write it out below.

_____

_____

_____

$\mathcal{A}$CT

1. Call to thank the person who spoke Scripture into your life in a power-packed way.

2. Call the person God used you to speak a power-packed scripture to. Follow up to see the long-term impact of God's Word.

3. Call the person God laid on your heart to share a scripture with (number 5 above).

4. Write out today's affirmation and scripture in your index-card notebook.

5. Write out your own prayer, expressing what God has shown you today about his mighty power.

_____

_____

_____

_____

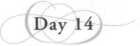

Do What Jesus Did

I tell you the truth, anyone who has faith in me will do
what I have been doing. He will do even greater things
than these, because I am going to the Father.

JOHN 14:12

W e have the Holy Spirit within us to help us become more and more like Jesus in terms of who we are. But God has also made divine provision for us to have the Holy Spirit upon us so we can do as Jesus did. When we experience the power of God, our lives should look remarkably similar to Jesus's. We are empowered to do what Jesus did.

In almost every instance in the Gospels, Jesus backed up his words with a demonstration of power. Sometimes it was the power to know the real issue at stake, as when he asked the invalid, "Do you want to get well?" (John 5:6). (Hey, some people like their infirmities—their identity is wrapped up in being sick!) At other times, Jesus spotted ulterior motives, as when the Pharisees tried to "catch him in his words" and "trap" him (see Mark 12:13–17). Other times, Jesus displayed his power to heal, feed thousands, calm storms, walk on water, and even raise the dead.

Jesus wasn't just a brilliant teacher. If that were the case, how would he be any different from Buddha or Muhammad? What most distinguished Jesus was not his insightful teachings but his actions. He didn't just tell people to believe his words. Quite the contrary. He said, in effect, "Believe what I do. Believe the works. Believe the miracles. Believe the demonstrations of divine power." He underscored this by saying, "Do not believe me unless I do what my Father does" (John 10:37). What makes Jesus different from all the other great teachers of world religions is that none of them came back from the dead. And the same power that raised Christ Jesus from the dead is alive and active in us. Or, it should be. Romans 8:11 tells us, "The Spirit of him who raised Jesus from the dead is living in you." Do you want to know why most of the world does not believe in Jesus? Because we, as his followers, do not do what Jesus did. Do you want to know which groups are advancing the gospel worldwide? Those who not only teach what Jesus taught, but who actually do what Jesus did.

Jesus said, "I tell you the truth, anyone who has faith in me will do what I have been doing. He will do even greater things than these, because I am going to the Father" (John 14:12). Could the verse be any more straightforward? We can dance around the verse all day long, but at midnight it will still say the same thing. It says that Jesus said anyone who has faith in him will do even greater things than he did. Anyone. Not just twelve guys in the first century. Anyone. Not just *might do. Will do.* It will happen. What will happen? Bible reading? Sunday-school teaching? Church-growth seminars? Does anyone believe that's what Jesus was talking about when he referenced "greater things"? You could hand the Bible to ten thousand random people who have no church background and ask them to read this passage—and not one of them would conclude that's what Jesus was talking about.

Some theologians have suggested that the word *greater* references "greater in number." For example, Christians can collectively feed far more than five thousand hungry people. World Vision, Food for the Hungry, and other international ministries feed countless thousands every day. That is certainly true, and it's always a miracle when someone is willing to sacrifice time and money to serve others. Christians have collectively shared the gospel with billions down through history—far more than Jesus did when he walked the dusty roads of ancient Palestine. We shouldn't minimize the miraculous significance of that.

However, Jesus said "he" not "they," so he clearly meant individual Christians would do greater things. Furthermore, the word rendered "greater" is the Greek word *mizon*. It occurs forty-five times in the New Testament, and in every instance refers to quality not quantity. Examine the verse in context: "At least believe on the evidence of the miracles themselves. I tell you the truth, anyone who has faith in me will do what I have been doing. [What had he been doing? Performing miracles!] He will do even greater things than these [what can "these" possibly be referencing other than the miracles?], because I am going to the Father. And I will do whatever you ask in my name, so that the Son may bring glory to the Father. You may ask me for anything in my name, and I will do it" (John 14:11–14).

That's what Jesus said. Personal experience is not the measure of truth; God's Word is the measure of truth. As we choose to believe his Word, he will show us his power. Does my experience line up with this passage? No. Not entirely. However, I have witnessed numerous miracles in recent years, not the least of which has been the salvation of approximately twenty-eight thousand people in Panama and Peru—led to Christ as part of a teen outreach ministry sponsored by Focus on the Family. Brio Missions reported that one team saw the multiplication of twenty peanut-butter-and-jelly sandwiches, which fed three hundred people with food left over.[11] Some would suggest the "even greater" miracle is that hundreds of teens would rather serve God than themselves, and I'm not sure I'd disagree.

Alas, there would be no story of three hundred people sharing twenty sandwiches—and having leftovers—if that group had responded to the situation with fear, rather than faith. Then again, good old-fashioned logic could have blocked a move of God just as effectively. What if this group had looked at the situation and concluded that since they couldn't feed everyone, there was no point in feeding anyone? No miracle would have occurred. Instead, they asked themselves, *What did Jesus do?* Then they did what Jesus did: they fed hundreds of people even though it was impossible to do so.

If we're not seeing miracles in our midst, I believe it's because we are unwilling to step out and do what Jesus did. Those teen missionaries experienced a miracle because they did not allow fear or logic to keep them from doing what Jesus did. That's what Jesus expected from his disciples, and it's what he expects from us. Some of us are so afraid of making a mistake or looking foolish that we never step out in faith. Jesus had no patience for that kind of attitude. He sent seventy-two of his followers out, telling them to pave the way for his coming and instructing them to heal the sick. "The seventy-two returned with joy and said, 'Lord, even the demons submit to us in your name'" (Luke 10:17). In response to their successful report, Jesus explained that it was because he had given them authority "to overcome all the power of the enemy" (Luke 10:19). The seventy-two had simply exercised the authority he had given them (see Day 27). Verse 21 tells us Jesus was "full of joy." Why? Because he'd found levelheaded followers who wouldn't make him look bad by trying anything radical and risking failure? No, he was full of joy because he'd found seventy-two people who were willing to step out and attempt to do the things he did.

The idea of being a rabbi's disciple was to become like the rabbi. When Jesus called disciples, he was calling people he wanted to train to become like him. Not only Jesus understood this; his disciples understood it too. That's why when Peter saw Jesus walking on the water, he believed walking on water might just be within his reach. Jesus didn't rebuke Peter for trying to imitate him; he didn't say walking on water was a stupid idea. Instead, Jesus reached his hand out just as Peter faltered, enabling him to succeed.

The disciples weren't the only ones who understood their role as ministry trainees; everyone else understood it too. A man with a demon-possessed son told Jesus, "I asked your disciples to drive out the spirit, but they could not" (Mark 9:18). Did you catch that? The man asked the disciples. Where did he get the idea that the disciples could do what Jesus did? They must have had a pretty good track record. Notice, too, that the disciples didn't tell the man he must be crazy to think they could do as Jesus did; instead, the disciples admitted they had tried…and failed.

Yet Jesus did not rebuke the disciples for attempting to imitate him. Quite the opposite. He told them how to be more effective in the future: "This kind can come forth by nothing, but by prayer and fasting" (Mark 9:29, KJV). Jesus sent his first disciples out into the world to minister, knowing that sometimes they would succeed and sometimes they would fail. Today, he sends us into the world, knowing the same about us.

When we step out to unleash God's power upon the world, we'll sometimes feel as if we're about to sink. Sometimes we'll try but fail. When that happens, we'll look and feel foolish. People might even be angry with us. They'll surely be disappointed, as the father of the demon-possessed son was. He went to the disciples' boss and complained about their job performance! Ouch! Does that mean we shouldn't try to do as Jesus did? Lots of sincere Christians obviously think so. They say we shouldn't risk looking foolish, because when we try but fail, it makes Jesus look bad. Well, guess what? Jesus could handle it two thousand years ago, and he can handle it today. All that matters to him is that we keep trying and remain teachable.

Here's something else to consider: even though the father complained about the disciples' ineffectiveness, it did not shake his faith in Jesus. More important, Jesus wanted to heal the man's son, so the son was healed. Something tells me the father soon forgot that his child wasn't healed the first time he asked.

You may think stepping out in faith to do the things Jesus did is risky, but nothing is riskier than disobedience. Jesus took risks. I mean, imagine him standing in front of Lazarus's tomb saying, "Come forth" (John 11:43, KJV) and nothing happens. Not getting the picture? Okay, go to the nearest cemetery where a funeral is in progress, walk up to the casket, and order the dead body to come forth. How foolish do you think you'll look if nothing happens? Of course, Jesus was able to eliminate all risk by hearing directly from the Father before opening his mouth. We can't eliminate risk, but we can minimize it if we, too, listen to the Father and act out of obedience to him.

Minimize. Not eliminate. We're children of God, but we're not the Son of God. Sometimes when you pray, the person you prayed for won't be healed. Sometimes you'll share a scripture or word of exhortation, and the listener will look at you like you're crazy. You'll show mercy and be met with contempt. You'll give and get taken advantage of. So what?

Peter took more risks than any of the other disciples. That's why it's so easy to pick on him and use him as sermon illustrations of what not to do. But when Peter got it right, he got it right big time. Who was the first to declare Jesus the Messiah? Who walked on water? Who was handed the keys to the kingdom? Who became the rock of the first-century church? The one who was willing to take the most risks and learn from his mistakes: Peter. You've got to get out there and try.

Exercising the power of God is like learning to walk. We all know babies fall and sometimes get hurt. One of the teachers at our local Christian school recently lost her toddler. The child simply fell, hit her head too hard...and died. Everyone was stunned by the news. But when I talked to my sister, who works at a large children's hospital in Philadelphia, she said, "You'd be surprised how many children get severely injured each year just by falling down." Should we not teach our babies to walk anymore because they might fall and get hurt? The very idea is ridiculous. Should you not imitate Jesus just because you will inevitably stumble from time to time? I hope you know the answer is no.

We are specifically given this command: "Be imitators of God, therefore, as dearly loved children" (Ephesians 5:1). Paul commended the Thessalonians, saying, "You became imitators of us and of the Lord," after he noted that "our gospel came to you not simply with words, but also with power" (1 Thessalonians 1:5–6). Jesus said all Christians must become like little children; actually, we begin as spiritual infants when we are born again (see John 3:3). Peter talked about us as infants needing spiritual milk (see 1 Peter 2:2). Clearly, God gets it. He knows we'll have to crawl before we walk. We'll stumble, but ultimately God wants us to "run with perseverance the race marked out for us" (Hebrews 12:1). The journey from crawling to running a marathon isn't an overnight trip; the key is having the courage to begin. If your goal is to run, you've got to start crawling.

Start by holding someone's hand while that person prays for the sick, simply agreeing in prayer. Then, someday, you'll have the courage to pray for the sick yourself. By the way, I'm talking about praying, as in actually expecting the person to get well.

Imitating Jesus is difficult, but it's not complicated. When Jesus encountered someone who was hungry—or even thousands of hungry people—he fed them. When he saw sick people, he healed them. Demon-possessed people? He cast out the demons. Religious people? He sought to shake them out of their complacency. Our mission is the same. We all know it. The challenge is to step out of the church pew and live it. The challenge is to become vessels of God's power.

Dear heavenly Father, forgive me for those times when fear or logic were more important to me than faith. Lord, just as the apostle Paul was willing to be a fool for Christ, so am I. I want to be like Peter, who was willing to risk getting it wrong, willing to risk failing. You have commanded me to be an imitator—to do what Jesus did. It's no longer enough for me to believe in the miracles Jesus performed. I'm ready to believe Jesus can do "even greater things" as I yield my life to become a vessel of God's power. Amen.

AFFIRM

I am an imitator of God.

APPLY

1. What do you think Jesus meant when he said, "I tell you the truth, anyone who has faith in me will do what I have been doing. He will do even greater things than these, because I am going to the Father"?

_____

_____

_____

2. Does your answer to question 1 reflect your conviction based on your study of God's Word *alone* or has your personal experience shaped your belief?

_____

_____

_____

3. What do you think the command, "Be imitators of God," means?

_____

_____

_____

4. When was the last time you imitated something Jesus *did*? What were the results?

_____

_____

_____

5. How does knowing you will inevitably stumble as you learn to be an imitator of God give you greater courage to step out in faith?

ᴀᴄᴛ

1. Think of one practical way you can imitate Jesus. Then do it.
2. Write out today's affirmation and scripture in your index-card notebook.
3. Write out your own prayer, expressing what God has shown you today about his mighty power.

Exercise Bold Faith

After they prayed, the place where they were meeting
was shaken. And they were all filled with the Holy
Spirit and spoke the word of God boldly.

ACTS 4:31

*W*hen I think of the way Jesus lived and how he conducted his
ministry, one of the first words that springs to mind is *boldness*.
Jesus made boldness a priority, and so did the early church, as we see in
the fourth chapter of the book of Acts. When Christians received the Holy
Spirit, they became bold: "After they prayed, the place where they were
meeting was shaken. And they were all filled with the Holy Spirit and
spoke the word of God boldly" (verse 31).

After Peter and John had healed a lame man, been thrown in prison,
and ordered never again to proclaim the name of Jesus, the church gathered together to pray. They didn't ask God to protect them from persecu-
tion. Instead they prayed, "Now, Lord, consider their threats and enable
your servants to speak your word with great boldness. Stretch out your
hand to heal and perform miraculous signs and wonders through the
name of your holy servant Jesus" (verses 29–30). Their concern was that,

in the face of threats and persecutions, they would have boldness to proclaim Christ and see him glorified.

We're also told that "Paul and Barnabas spent considerable time [in Iconium], speaking boldly for the Lord, who confirmed the message of his grace by enabling them to do miraculous signs and wonders" (Acts 14:3). Paul acted boldly, he spoke boldly, and he *wrote* boldly. Even when Paul was under house arrest in Rome, "Boldly and without hindrance he preached the kingdom of God and taught about the Lord Jesus Christ" (Acts 28:31). Considering the extraordinary fruitfulness of Paul's life and ministry, I would say God was well pleased with his bold approach.

I believe the Holy Spirit favors the bold rather than the timid. Timidity may seem the considerate or even spiritual approach, but the Bible states "God did not give us a spirit of timidity" (2 Timothy 1:7). The Message Bible puts it this way: "God doesn't want us to be shy with his gifts, but bold."

William Carey lived by the motto: "Expect great things from God; attempt great things for God."[12] At the time, the church had (with few exceptions) ignored the Great Commission for a thousand years. In 1792, Carey had the nerve to publish a book challenging Christians to own up to their long-neglected responsibilities to boldly take the gospel to all nations. Fellow pastors vigorously opposed him when he tried to establish the first overseas missionary agency. At one meeting a leader snapped at him: "Young man, sit down. When God pleases to convert the heathen, he'll do it without consulting you or me."[13]

When Carey and his wife left everything to take the gospel to India, people thought he was insane. Once there, three of their children died, and his wife really *did* lose her sanity. What must people have thought then? I have a dear friend on the mission field who is under siege because her unmarried daughter became pregnant. People are telling her, "Come home! This missions business is hurting your kids!" Imagine what people said of the risks Carey took, not only with his own life, but the lives of his family members.

But he pressed on. His team founded nineteen mission stations, numerous churches, and one hundred schools in India (with a total enrollment of ten thousand). They translated Scripture into thirty-four languages and produced grammars and dictionaries still used today. And they organized India's first medical mission, savings bank, seminary, girls' school, and vernacular newspaper.[14] His life and work inspired tens of thousands to go to the mission field. To this day, Carey is highly revered throughout India.

The Old Testament book of Daniel contains the story of three teenagers who demonstrated great boldness. The armies of King Nebuchadnezzar captured Shadrach, Meshach, and Abednego and dragged them away to Babylon. When the king built a gold idol and commanded everyone to bow down and worship it, the three refused, even though they knew the punishment was death. When the king demanded an explanation, they declared, "O Nebuchadnezzar, we do not need to defend ourselves before you in this matter. If we are thrown into the blazing furnace, the God we serve is able to save us from it, and he will rescue us from your hand, O king. But even if he does not, we want you to know, O king, that we will not serve your gods or worship the image of gold you have set up" (Daniel 3:16–18).

That's bold faith! Bold because they knew God was able to demonstrate power; faith because even if God chose not to deliver them from death, they would remain unshaken. Like William Carey, these three young men expected great things from God, therefore God empowered them to do great things for him.

Many Bible scholars believe the faith of these young men was rewarded with a visitation from Jesus. Others believe it was an angel. We're told only that there was a fourth man in the fire with them, who looked like "a son of the gods" (Daniel 3:25). In either case, the three bold men were not only unbowed, they were "unbound and unharmed" (verse 25). The only thing they lost in the fire was their chains. Afterward, the king even promoted them. Of course, none of those miracles would have happened if Shadrach, Meshach, and Abednego had decided to go along to get along, if they had chosen to do what we're often tempted to do: blend in with the crowd. God promises that when we walk through the fire, he will be with us. Unfortunately, many of us miss the opportunity to experience God walking with us—and miss out on promotions, as well—because we are unwilling to exercise such bold faith.

The boldest person I have met is Hector Torres, founder of Hispanic International Ministries.[15] Latin Americans know his name, as do people in my home church, which happens to have been his home church for the last twenty-five years. The first time I heard Hector speak, he ended his message by offering to pray for anyone who needed "a word from God." Hundreds of people went forward...including me. Hector prayed for people in the front row, then suddenly pressed through the crowd to where I was standing about five rows back. He put his hand on my head and prayed exactly what I needed to hear. He identified the precise issue that had compelled me to go forward. Since he prayed right into a microphone, all of my friends heard, were blown away, and came rushing over to hold me as I collapsed in a river of tears.

Hector had never met me, had no idea who I was, and I had not spoken one word to him. He simply walked over and prayed boldly. Lest you're thinking, *Well, he probably prayed lots of things and accidentally got one thing right.* Wrong. He prayed four brief sentences: he covered the situation, God's perspective concerning it, God's proposed solution, and God's promise that he would bring about the solution.

Prayer done. Then Hector went on and prayed for the next person with equal boldness.

Is it right to pray with such boldness? Jesus said it is. In response to the disciples' request that he teach them how to pray, Jesus told the story of the persistent friend and noted, "I tell you, though he will not get up and give him the bread because he is his friend, yet *because of the man's boldness* he will get up and give him as much as he needs" (Luke 11:8, emphasis added).

When I learned that Hector would again be preaching and praying for people, I mentioned it to my teenage daughter. When I picked her up from school on the appointed day (a Friday), the first words out of her mouth weren't, "Hi, Mom"; they were, "Are we going to hear Hector tonight?"

We sure did. And my normally very shy daughter was the first person up for prayer. Again, Hector prayed with great boldness and, without speaking to my daughter, he precisely identified her needs and God's answer to them. He specifically mentioned that God had appointed her to be an Esther.

This story gets better.

When we returned to our seats, Leah was sobbing, and a few of my friends rallied around her. One prayed—mentioning Esther. Leah then decided to go forward to another woman who was helping Hector pray for people. I know this woman well and consider her a mighty prayer warrior. She, too, mentioned Esther in her prayer. Hector had *not* preached about Esther that evening, not even remotely. Nor had either of these women overheard his prayer for Leah. Instead, all three were boldly praying the words God had placed in their mouths.

The next morning, we found Leah curled up in our family prayer room with a Bible on her lap, opened to the book of Esther. Hector's boldness—and the boldness of the other prayer warriors—made a profound impact on Leah. Months later, she is still talking about Esther. Such is the power of bold prayers. Such is the power of bold faith.

⟨⟋⟩

Dear heavenly Father, I want to exercise bold faith. I want to live as Jesus lived. I know that in becoming bolder, I'll also be taking more risks. Even as you had to occasionally rebuke Peter and get him back in line, I know that sometimes I may overstep my bounds, and you may have to rebuke me as well. Holy Spirit, I trust you to be my mentor as I endeavor to develop bold faith. Teach me where we shall begin, whether it's issuing bold invitations for people to come to church, asking bold questions to open dialogue with unbelievers, praying boldly, or boldly expecting miracles. I'm ready for the next step on this journey, whatever it might be. Amen.

AFFIRM

God has called me to exercise bold faith.

APPLY

1. Are you naturally bold or timid? Give examples.

_____

_____

_____

2. What was your reaction to some of the examples of bold faith shared in this chapter?

_____

_____

_____

3. Who is the boldest Christian you know? Describe the outcome of their approach.

_____

_____

_____

4. Describe the boldest thing you've ever done (for the kingdom!) and the results.

_____

_____

_____

5. In what area of your life do you believe the Holy Spirit is direct-
ing you to exhibit more boldness? What steps of obedience do
you plan to take in response?

_____

_____

_____

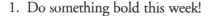

ACT

1. Do something bold this week!
2. Write out today's affirmation and scripture in your index-card
notebook.
3. Write out your own prayer, expressing what God has shown you
today about his mighty power.

_____

_____

_____

_____

Realize God Wants to Say Yes

The prayer offered in faith will make the sick person well; the Lord will raise him up. If he has sinned, he will be forgiven. Therefore confess your sins to each other and pray for each other so that you may be healed. The prayer of a righteous man is powerful and effective.

JAMES 5:15–16

My friend Sherman saw his first dramatic yes answer to prayer while serving an eight-year prison term for arson. Immediately upon arriving in prison, he noticed that all his fellow inmates belonged to various groups. There was the group that played cards, the group that worked out, the group plotting various jailhouse scams—but the group that caught Sherman's attention was always laughing, always positive and enthusiastic, which, of course, made no sense, as they were in prison. So one day, Sherman approached this group in the prison yard, sat down, and listened in. The men were talking about Jesus. One man said, "I may be behind walls, I may be behind bars, but I am a free man!"

Sherman knew immediately he needed Jesus. He reached out for help and prayed his first real prayer, asking Jesus to set him free. He was instantly filled with the same overwhelming joy and laughter. When his fellow inmates handed him a Bible so he could join in their study, Sherman's heart sank: he didn't know how to read. Back in his cell, he clutched the Bible to his chest and offered up his second prayer: *Dear God, I'm desperate to learn about you. I want to read this book, but you know I can't. Please help me.* Within days, Sherman was enrolled in a literacy class, where he astonished everyone with how quickly he learned to read. He says it was nothing short of miraculous.

Several months later, Sherman was lying on his cot late at night when it occurred to him that he was ready to tell his family and friends how God had completely transformed his life. He prayed, *Dear Jesus, I want to serve you on the streets. I can't do that from in here.* The next morning, guards arrived at his cell unexpectedly, informing him that he was due in court. On the way, one of them told him, "You're getting out of here today." Within hours, Sherman was indeed a free man. No bond. No parole. Nothing. Free. After serving only eight months of his sentence. No explanation was ever given for his release. Those events occurred nearly forty years ago. Today, Sherman is in his seventies. He is the most joyous, vibrant person you will ever meet. He has more energy than most twenty-year-olds. And he continues to see miraculous answers to prayer as he ministers on the streets of Phoenix.

We shouldn't be surprised that Sherman's prayers were so powerful and effective. We should be surprised that our prayers are *not.* The Bible says, "The prayer of a righteous man is powerful and effective" (James 5:16). So if our prayers are *not* powerful and have *no effect,* shouldn't we ask why? Many Christians respond in one of three ways when they don't see God answering yes to their prayers, and I believe each of these ways cripples our faith and blocks God's power.

One, we assume God is the cause for a no answer. A far more likely explanation is that we are the cause—perhaps our prayers are out of alignment with God's stated will, or maybe we have unconfessed sin. Another cause could be that we have prayed a generic prayer instead of a specific prayer. If we restrict ourselves to praying, *God bless everyone,* we are not in alignment with God's Word, which unmistakably states that our prayers should be powerful enough to cause drought (see 1 Kings 17:1), bring down fire from heaven (see 1 Kings 18:38; 2 Kings 1:10–14; 1 Chronicles 21:26; 2 Chronicles 7:1), or toss a mountain into the sea (see Mark 11:23).

Two, we explain it away by saying that God gave us something better instead, such as patience. I have a problem with this rationale, because in Matthew 7:9–11, Jesus said he would *not* answer specific prayers by giving us *something else* instead of what we ask for: "Which of you, if his son asks for bread, will give him a stone? Or if he asks for a fish, will give him a snake? If you, then, though you are evil, know how to give good gifts to your children, how much more will your Father in heaven give good gifts to those who ask him!" Jesus also said, "Ask and it will be given to you; seek and you will find; knock and the door will be opened to you. For everyone who asks receives; he who seeks finds; and to him who knocks, the door will be opened" (Matthew 7:7–8).

Third, we give up too soon, assuming God's answer is no. One day when I was struggling to understand why so many of my prayers for specific circumstances were going unanswered, a friend said, "All prayer is answered, but sometimes the answer is no." Although I knew what she meant and realized she was technically correct, I also believe that line of thinking hinders our effectiveness in prayer. While sometimes God does say no, the clear teaching and example of Scripture is that he much prefers to say yes. Yet too often, we give up praying before we get to yes!

God wants to say yes to our prayers. That's why he instructs us to pray. But if we don't get a yes immediately, we say, "Well, God must have said no to that one...and that one...and that one...and that one." Some of us think God is like those hilarious commercials about trying to redeem frequent flyer miles—no matter what the customer asks, the answer is *no*! Or we see God sitting up in heaven with a giant rubber stamp: no, *no*, NO!

God did not create prayer as an exercise in futility. He created prayer as a tool to bring heaven's power to bear upon the affairs of earth. For example:

- We read in Exodus how God answered many of Moses's prayers in miraculous ways, including parting the Red Sea (see 14:13–22) and giving the Israelites good water in the wilderness (see 15:25). His prayer even persuaded God to "change his mind" and spare Israel after the golden-calf affair (see 32:7–14).
- God answered Elijah's prayer on Mt. Carmel when he rained fire from heaven in the battle against the prophets of Baal (see 1 Kings 18:20–40).
- Daniel was a mighty man of prayer who experienced many powerful answers. In response to prayer, God revealed the king's undisclosed dream to Daniel (see Daniel 2:17–19). God shut the lions' mouths (see 6:4–24).
- Hezekiah prayed for protection against Sennacherib's army, and God wiped out 185,000 enemy troops while the Israelites slept (see 2 Kings 19).

- Jonah prayed to be delivered from the belly of the fish, and God caused it to spit him out on dry land (see Jonah 2).

Clearly, God delights in saying yes to our prayers! We'll spend the next several days taking a look at how we can maximize the power and effectiveness of our prayers.

Dear heavenly Father, I thank you for giving me prayer as a powerful tool to bring the reality of heaven to bear upon the circumstances that surround me. Forgive me for my lackadaisical attitude toward prayer; for my unwillingness to consider that the problem of unanswered prayers does not lie with you, but with me. You are not an ineffective God, but too often my prayers are powerless and ineffective. I'm so thankful that you are eager to say yes to my prayers. Holy Spirit, teach me to pray with power and effectiveness. Amen.

AFFIRM

I believe God likes to say yes to my prayers.

APPLY

1. What do you think is the purpose of prayer? Support your
   answer.

   _____

   _____

   _____

2. Can you identify with any of the reasons why our prayers go
   unanswered? Explain your answer.

   _____

   _____

   _____

3. How do you respond to the point that God likes to say yes to
   our prayers?

   _____

   _____

   _____

4. Describe a time when you prayed a specific prayer and received
   a specific response. What impact did that have on your faith and
   the faith of those around you?

   _____

   _____

   _____

5. Note some specific prayer concerns.

_____

_____

_____

ACT

1. Begin to pray specifically and expect specific answers.
2. Write out today's affirmation and scripture in your index-card notebook.
3. Write out your own prayer, expressing what God has shown you today about his mighty power.

_____

_____

_____

_____

Root Your Prayers in Scripture

Jesus said to him, "Away from me, Satan!
For it is written..."

MATTHEW 4:10

At the dedication service for her daughter Amy, Beth chose a life verse: "The beloved of the LORD shall dwell in safety" (Deuteronomy 33:12, KJV). Each night as she tucked her little one into bed—and often throughout the day—she would pray this scripture over Amy. Then early one morning, Beth's wood stove caught on fire. While she busily tossed water on the fire in her family room, she failed to realize that the second floor was engulfed in flames and that her toddler was in grave danger. Suddenly, a man appeared, walked directly into the burning house, and pulled Beth and Amy out unharmed. Then the man immediately disappeared. No one had ever seen him before or since. Beth has no doubt that God answered her daily prayers by sending an angel.

At the time of the fire, Beth was seven months pregnant with her daughter Linda. Fast forward several decades. Following her mother's godly example, each night Linda prayed a hedge of protection for her children. One hot autumn afternoon, Linda put her two-year-old son, Juden, down for a nap. Since her husband had not yet installed the window-unit air conditioner for the summer, Linda decided to open the window. When Juden woke up, he looked out the window and saw his father coming home from a bike ride. He pushed on the screen, falling eighteen feet to the ground below. To the left of where he landed were concrete steps; to the right, the metal air-conditioning unit. Miraculously, Juden fell right between the steps and the air conditioner; had he not, he almost certainly would have died. His parents rushed him to the hospital. To everyone's astonishment, the doctors could find nothing wrong with Juden. Not one bruise, cut, or scratch. No injury whatsoever. Still, the doctors insisted on keeping him nearly a week for observation, certain that something must be wrong. Juden was released, whole and unharmed, on Easter morning. Linda recounts the experience:

I was weepy and frazzled and incredibly paranoid; it seemed like everywhere I looked, I saw a potential danger. I realized that although I was so thankful for Juden's safety, I could not be at peace with the guilt of what could have been. I kept telling myself I was entrusted with this child whom I had failed to protect. I failed to foresee danger and perhaps even caused it. I was questioning everything about my identity as a mom, my very highest calling. I felt like the worst mother in the world.

What happened next is something I will forever hold precious in my heart as one of the little signs God sends to remind us of his gentle love and care. I wandered over and stood under Juden's window. It was painful to bring myself to look up. Then something caught my eye, and as I knelt down, I saw a tiny sparrow where Juden had fallen. I started to cry and at that moment I felt like God said to me, *I saw this sparrow fall, and I saw Juden fall. And I held him.*

The sparrow was a very meaningful symbol to me. "His Eye Is on the Sparrow" was one of my father's favorite hymns and also one of mine. I whispered that phrase in my dad's ear on more than one occasion while I watched him battle the cancer that took him from us less than two years ago. I had sung it to Juden many a night. The hymn is based on Matthew 10:29: "Are not two sparrows sold for a farthing? and one of them shall not fall to the ground without your Father." What a powerful reminder of a God who cares for every little creation and how much more he cares for and loves us. God spoke peace to me through a tiny bird. Every time I see one, I am reminded of the day God held my son and gave him back to me.

I wish I could say that I learned early to root my prayers in Scripture as Beth and Linda did. But for years my prayers were a litany of complaints to God. I had read Psalms and noted that David didn't hesitate to vent his frustration with God, yet he is regarded as a man after God's own heart. So venting was all I ever did in prayer. I hadn't yet noticed that after David poured out his complaints, he then poured out praise to God and expressed his confidence in God's character. I failed to recognize the countless times David recalled the power and promises of God to deliberately remind himself that no matter how bad the situation might look, God is greater still.

Not only did I vent when I prayed, but I also let my mind wander and would fall asleep during prayer. I'd set the timer for thirty minutes and think, *Okay, today I'm going to become a mighty prayer warrior. Today, I'm going to pray for a half hour. Don't* tell me you've never done that!

Within minutes, I'd suddenly realize I was thinking about the day's schedule, or a phone call I needed to make, or someone who had hurt my feelings the day before, or…or…or! Even worse, the bell would ding…and wake me up! Then I'd beat myself up, bemoaning the fact that I was such a lightweight prayer and a lousy excuse for a Christian.

After attending a prayer conference, I decided the key to overcoming my powerless prayers was writing them out rather than simply praying silently in my head. So I began writing out a daily litany of complaints. The seminar leader had also mentioned the importance of confession, so each day I would also write a long list of everything that was wrong with me. Day after day I lamented my selfishness, my lack of spiritual power, my character flaws and inability to overcome entrenched sins. You can well imagine what an uplifting exercise this was! Yet, I couldn't figure out why my prayers were still powerless.

One day, as I scribbled the same list of complaints, sins, and character flaws, I overheard a heavenly *harrumph*. God had my attention! I knew a rebuke was coming: *You call this prayer?* the Holy Spirit questioned. *This isn't prayer; this is a gripe-and-groan session.* For the next hour, I read through page after page of my prayers desperately scribbled down in notebook after notebook. If sheer volume of words was enough to unleash the power of God, I should have been Billy Graham by then. My approach to prayer wasn't working, and there was just no denying it.

Around that time, I began taking a Kay Arthur study offered through a local church. I marveled at the wisdom, peace, and quiet confidence oozing from our class leader, Helen. When she prayed, everyone felt uplifted. Her prayers were unlike any I had ever heard before: her soft voice overpowered the room with a holy boldness that astonished me. Her words were not merely her own; her words were the words of God, as she incorporated scripture after scripture into her prayers. I asked Helen if she would teach me what God had taught her about prayer. She graciously invited me into her home and spent hours teaching me about the power of praying God's Word.

To pray Scripture, simply open your Bible, search out passages you've highlighted, and turn them into prayers. For example, my life verse is 2 Corinthians 4:7: "We have this treasure in jars of clay to show that this all-surpassing power is from God and not from us." Here's how I might turn this verse into a prayer:

Heavenly Father, I acknowledge that I am merely a jar of clay. You know my faults and weaknesses better than I do myself, because you are the one who made me. Therefore, I'm not going to beat myself up today. Instead, I'm going to trust you to bring to my attention those things in my life and character that you want to remold. Thanks for being such a wonderful, faithful potter. I trust you. You're going to make me everything you want me to be, if I'll simply cooperate with you. Lord, how can I ever thank you enough for depositing the priceless treasure of the Holy Spirit within me. Wow! The same Spirit that raised Christ Jesus from the dead is alive and active in me. I stand amazed. Father, I want to show forth your power today. Make it obvious that the power is from you, not from me. I don't want to do anything that might draw people to me; help me to point them to you. God, it's all about you. Thank you for setting your love upon me; help me to demonstrate that love to the people I meet today. Amen.

When we root our prayers in Scripture, we can pray with power-packed faith, because we know our prayers are in alignment with God's will. Praying the Bible is an acquired skill that improves with practice. You can begin by praying aloud from a book of Scripture prayers. I love to sit in our family prayer chapel, reading prayers aloud. My favorite right now is *Prayers That Avail Much* by Germaine Copeland. Let me also recommend my book *Becoming the Woman I Want to Be*. It not only includes Scripture prayers, but it also walks you through the process of turning Scripture into prayer and gives you ninety days of practice in writing out your own. Many readers have reported that this process has enabled them to experience the power of God in fresh, new ways.

If you want to experience real power in prayer, pray God's Word.

～

Dear heavenly Father, the power and purpose of your Word never ceases to amaze me. Thank you that I cannot only read your Word, but can use it to empower my prayers. There are no words to express my gratitude for this unspeakable gift. Teach me to pray Scripture so I can be certain my prayers are in accordance with your will. Amen.

AFFIRM

Praying God's Word unleashes God's power in my life.

APPLY

1. Could you identify with any of the frustrations with prayer mentioned in today's readings? Describe.

_____

_____

_____

2. Who has been the greatest influence on your prayer life? Explain.

_____

_____

_____

3. What are some most significant lessons you've learned about praying effectively?

_____

_____

_____

4. Describe a turning point in your understanding of or experience with prayer.

_____

_____

_____

5. What practical steps can you take to increase your skill at praying Scripture-based prayers?

_____

_____

_____

ACT

1. Purchase one or more books filled with Scripture-based prayers.
2. Write out your own Scripture-based prayers and pray them aloud.
3. Write out today's affirmation and scripture in your index-card notebook.
4. Write out your own prayer, expressing what God has shown you today about his mighty power.

_____

_____

_____

_____

Open Yourself
to God-Prompted Prayer

Elijah was a man just like us. He prayed
earnestly that it would not rain, and it did not
rain on the land for three and a half years.

JAMES 5:17

Several years ago, Mark and his wife signed up for a church tour billed as an opportunity to walk in the footsteps of the apostle Paul. The three-week journey included a visit to the ancient city of Ephesus, Turkey, where people once rioted in objection to Paul's preaching, chanting, "Great is Artemis of the Ephesians!" (Acts 19:28). Having studied the book of Ephesians and the history surrounding it in preparation for the trip, Mark was familiar with the statue of Artemis and the spiritual forces it represented.

But nothing prepared him for the moment when he came face to face with a twenty-foot-tall, exact replica of the statue. It was situated at the entrance to the main street in a bustling city filled with quaint shops, restaurants, and outdoor cafés, where overhanging trees and bright flowers made for a breathtaking view. Yet all Mark could see was darkness. He recalls, "The best way I can describe the atmosphere was oppressive. Everything seemed gray."

As Mark began walking around the statue, he felt indignation rising up within him. Jesus had died to defeat *all* the forces of darkness and *all* idols, and that certainly included Artemis. Paul had risked his life to bring these people the truth two thousand years earlier. Suddenly, Mark knew with everything within him that Artemis *had to go*, and that God was calling *him* to pray for God's will to be done concerning the statue. Notice that Mark didn't start praying from a prayer list. He started praying *at God's prompting*. God told Mark something that was on *God's* heart, rather than vice versa, as we often pray.

While the rest of the tour group shopped and dined, Mark prayed. He says, "I knew God was telling me it wasn't his will for that statue to remain where it was. It had been torn down in heaven because of the cross, so it had no right to stand on that street corner, either." Mark and his wife thought the journey would end when they returned to the United States, but instead, Mark's spiritual journey was just beginning. He couldn't shake the statue of Artemis. Each day, as he ran on his treadmill, he continued to feel a burden to pray. So he kept praying…and praying…and praying.

Almost a year later, Mark joined a prayer team going through Turkey on an intercessory journey. When he arrived at the site where the statue had stood, it was gone. He says, "I was shocked. Even though I had been praying for almost a year, and I know God's Word can never return void, I still found it unbelievable!" In its place was a beautiful, peaceful garden featuring grass and red flowers. Mark couldn't help thinking that the green symbolized the life Jesus came to bring and that the red was a reminder of the price Jesus paid. "The atmosphere was completely different," he recalls. "The little garden was very peaceful." Peaceful. Just like the Prince of Peace. When Mark asked local shopkeepers what had happened to the statue, they said the city had taken it away for refurbishing. Then they added, "You never know. A lot of times they start these projects but never finish. Maybe the statue won't ever come back." Well, that's exactly what Mark is praying!

Here's a question worth pondering: If God wanted that statue removed, why didn't he just remove it? Why involve Mark? Why prompt him to pray? Why burden Mark to pray, day after day, month after month? Here's something else to think about: The Bible says that "Elijah was a man just like us. He prayed earnestly that it would not rain, and it did not rain on the land for three and a half years" (James 5:17). What if Elijah hadn't prayed earnestly? Would the outcome have changed? If the drought was God's idea, why didn't God just prevent the rain from falling? Why involve Elijah? Why did Elijah have to pray so earnestly? Why does God commend Elijah's prayers, crediting them with preventing rain for three years? Isn't God the ruler of the heavens? Isn't he the one who sends—or refuses to send—rain? Wasn't it God's idea to send a three-year drought in the first place? Did you ever think about that, or is it just me?

Is it possible that Elijah's prayers were essential? Is it possible that when Jesus commanded us to *pray* for his kingdom to come and his will to be done that there was more to it than just keeping Christians busy with a religious activity? Is it possible that if we *don't pray* for God's kingdom to come and his will to be done, we can *hinder* God's kingdom? The truth is, many of us think prayer is nice…but not necessary. We would never say that aloud, of course. But deep inside, many Christians believe that God's kingdom will come and his will shall be done *whether or not* we pray. Maybe that's why only one in ten thousand American Christians prays for an hour a day.[16] We simply don't believe our prayers are essential. But if that is the case, what is the purpose of prayer?

Over the years, I have noticed a trend. Unlike the human-generated prayer-list prayers we pray that never seem to get answered, prayer requests that come directly from God's heart to ours—promptings that come in the middle of the night or out of nowhere, promptings to pray for things we weren't even thinking about—*those* prayers get the most dramatic and often immediate results. For example, one woman was sitting in her living room watching television when God told her to get on her knees and pray for her sister-in-law. Completely unknown to the woman, at that very instant her brother was loading a shotgun. He walked into his bedroom and fired it point-blank at his wife...and missed.[17]

Betty Culley awoke during the night from a dream about an old friend from high school and felt strongly that she should pray for her. She recalls, "I wrote my friend the next morning, telling her about how God had placed her heavily on my heart and that I had prayed for her. She didn't respond for a couple of weeks, and I began to think it had been just a dream with no spiritual meaning. When I did hear from my friend, I learned that she and her husband had been on a trip to Russia, and at the very time I was praying for her, she had fallen in Red Square and received a serious concussion. She had pretty much recovered from it when she wrote and said that she had felt very much the presence of God during the ordeal and in her healing."

As I started paying attention to the issue of self-initiated prayer versus God-prompted prayer, I began to hear story after story just like these. I was determined to understand *why such prayers are so tremendously effective*. Then one day, I heard God say, *Because I have the real prayer list*. We've been getting it backward all along. We think our job is to look around and make notes concerning what's wrong in the world. Then we go to God and tell him what needs to be done to make things right—or at least, more to our liking. Wrong! Our primary role in prayer is *praying what God directs us to pray.* We pray about matters on *his* prayer list. Although I don't pretend to understand why, the more I study Scripture and church history, the more convinced I become that God's acting is contingent upon our asking. When he wants to *intervene* in human affairs, his eyes range throughout all the earth, searching for someone who will *intercede,* thereby inviting him to act. I believe God actively seeks prayer partners. When he finds a listening ear, he shares what's on his heart and invites that person to agree with him in prayer.

I once spoke at a women's retreat where the theme was FROG: Fully Relying on God. I prayed earnestly about the theme, asking God to show me how to encourage and strengthen the women in attendance to rely on him. But the Holy Spirit told me, *Tell them I am glad they want to fully rely on me, but I need to be able to fully rely on them too.* Paul likened the relationship between Jesus and the church to marriage (see Ephesians 5:22–33). It's not enough for the wife to rely on her husband; the husband has to be able to rely on his wife as well. It's not enough for us as Christians to rely on Jesus as our husband; he must be able to rely on us to be his faithful bride. Faithful in what? Among other things, faithful in prayer. Jesus relied on his first disciples to carry out the work of his kingdom, and he still relies on his church today. Can he rely on you?

I'm not saying we have to throw away our prayer lists, but I will say this: far better to come before God with a blank notebook, humbly asking: *Dear Father, what's on your prayer list today?* That's one prayer I guarantee God will answer. If you want to see God's power at work, discover the joy of God-directed prayer.

⟽

Dear heavenly Father, thank you for granting me the unspeakable privilege of being your prayer partner. Wow! Forgive me for coming

to you with my own agenda, my own list of demands, and calling
it a prayer list. I want to know what's on your heart so I can partner
with you by praying for your kingdom to come and your will
to be done, right here on earth, as it is in heaven. Holy Spirit, I'm
here, available and willing to pray whatever you want me to pray.
Burden me with the prayer requests that are nearest to your heart.
I look forward to experiencing your power as I witness dramatic
responses to those prayers that you prompt me to pray. Amen.

AFFIRM

I believe there's power in God-directed prayer.

APPLY

1. What evidence do you see in Scripture that believers have a vital
   role in prayer?

   _____

   _____

   _____

2. Have you ever been so focused on your own prayer list that you haven't even considered that God might have his own prayer list? What was the impact of that focus?

_____

_____

_____

3. In your experience (in both your personal life and church), how effective are human-generated prayer lists?

_____

_____

_____

4. Describe your own experience with God-directed prayer—a time when you felt prompted, even burdened, to pray for a particular person or situation. What was the result?

_____

_____

_____

5. How can you make yourself more open to God-directed prayer? Be as practical as possible in your response.

_____

_____

_____

ACT

1. Put your prayer list away, at least for a season. Instead, take out a blank notebook, and for the next month or more, come to God each morning and say, *Lord, what's on your prayer list today?*
2. Write out today's affirmation and scripture in your index-card notebook.
3. Write out your own prayer, expressing what God has shown you today about his mighty power.

_____

_____

_____

_____

Pray with Others

Where two or three are gathered together in my name,
there am I in the midst of them.

MATTHEW 18:20, KJV

O ne of the most spiritual places I've ever been was a centuries-old Spanish monastery. It was truly holy ground. God's presence permeated the place, and whenever two or three people were gathered for prayer, he spoke clearly and unmistakably. I can't wait to get to heaven, so I can meet the monk who prayed the prayers and cried the tears to hallow that ground. It was absolutely awe inspiring.

One day I went into the small chapel, alone and eager to hear from God. Nothing happened. God said nothing. Nada. Thirty minutes passed. Still nothing. Then a stranger walked in and sat quietly in the back. The minute she walked in, God's presence became palpable to me once again, but I still wasn't hearing from him. I desperately needed to experience his power in that moment. So I mounted the courage to ask the woman, "Would you be willing to pray with me?" She didn't look at me as if I were crazy, so that was a good sign! She took my hands, we bowed our heads together, and although she didn't utter a word, God immediately began speaking to me.

The difference was so dramatic that I knew God was trying to show me something. Then God whispered, *Two or three. Where two or three are gathered together in my name, there am I in the midst of them.*

While we can certainly unleash God's power when we pray alone, Scripture tells us there is a time for corporate prayer. Have you ever noticed that when the disciples asked Jesus to teach them how to pray, he instructed them to say, "Our Father...forgive us our debts..."? Read it for yourself:

This, then, is how you should pray:

"Our Father in heaven,
hallowed be your name,
your kingdom come,
your will be done
*   on earth as it is in heaven.*
Give us today our daily bread.
Forgive us our debts,
*   as we also have forgiven our debtors.*
And lead us not into temptation,
but deliver us from the evil one." (Matthew 6:9–13)

Did you notice all the plural pronouns: *us, we, our*? I didn't either! Not until I heard Daniel Henderson, pastor and author of *Fresh Encounters,* speaking on prayer.[18] If Jesus were telling us to pray privately, why did he use plural pronouns? Did he have bad grammar? Or did he think all those men were suffering from multiple personality disorder (you've got to wonder about Peter, but...)? Think about it: do you refer to yourself in first-person plural? Let's hope not. The clear implication is this: Jesus was saying, *If you want to know the most effective way to pray, the answer is corporately.* When Jesus said, "This, then, is how you should pray," he used the plural form of *you.* He didn't say, "This is how you, individually, should pray." He said, "This is how you, as a group of believers, should pray." If he'd been from the South, he would have said, "When ya'll pray…"

But wait, you protest, didn't Jesus withdraw to quiet places to pray alone? He sure did. But in Gethsemane, he was looking for prayer partners and was profoundly disappointed when no one was up to the task. There's a time for solitary prayer and a time for corporate prayer. A time for private prayer and a time for public prayer. A time to pray silently and a time to pray aloud.

However, the majority of Western Christians believe the secret to power in prayer is to pray in secret. But does the Bible teach this? I thought so; but again, Henderson caused me to reconsider. He explains that the Greek word rendered "closet" is *tamieon,* which refers to an inner chamber or important meeting room in a castle, a place where the king met with his most trusted advisors to discuss issues of significance.[19]

Henderson goes on to say that the Western approach to prayer has much more to do with our obsession with rugged individualism than the example of Scripture. You may also be surprised to learn that Christians in other parts of the world do not place the same emphasis on private prayer. Many of our brothers and sisters in Africa and Asia take a different approach. They believe what Tertullian said in the second century: "We come together for a meeting in order to besiege God with prayers, like an army in battle formation."[20] While not ignoring private prayer, they value corporate prayer. They not only pray together, they pray together aloud and simultaneously! I've experienced this form of unified prayer. The sound is both deafening and life changing. There's definitely a sense that the heavens are under siege!

Unfortunately, corporate prayer has gotten a bad rap in the West. It brings to mind visions of a handful of die-hard, elderly saints with nothing better to do on a Wednesday night. Even in megachurches, where thousands of people attend Sunday-morning services, it's not unusual for less than twenty people to show up for weekly prayer meetings. Some churches have even removed the weekly prayer meeting from their calendars. I heard one pastor explain, from the pulpit, that the board had decided to permanently eliminate it because it conflicted with too many sporting events and extracurricular activities. He said weekly prayer meetings no longer fit in with the American lifestyle and that the church had to keep up with the times.

He was serious.

Of course, having attended some of those prayer meetings, I have to admit: the cancellation was no great loss. Although I could never put my finger on why, I had found church prayer meetings extremely frustrating. They always went something like this: the pastor or small group leader would say, "Does anyone have any prayer requests?" Then, for the next ten, twenty, thirty, or sixty minutes, we'd talk about ourselves and our problems. The truly magnanimous, selfless saints would raise their hands and request prayer for their next-door neighbor's cousin's mother's brother-in-law's Uncle Bob from Kansas who, at the tender age of ninety-seven, had been tragically stricken with heart failure. When no more hands were raised, the group leader would announce it was time to pray. Our sentence-or-two prayers typically went something like this: "Dear God, I just pray for Uncle Bob. Please just do whatever you're going to do because we just know that you are in control and you just always do whatever you just want to do no matter what we do. Amen." Hey, that's the kind of prayer I prayed, too, so I'm not casting stones here! Five minutes later, the group's leader would declare a decisive "Amen." And I'd think, *There's got to be more to corporate prayer than this.* But of course, I had no idea what.

So I began searching out corporate prayer in Scripture. One of the most striking examples occurs during the reign of King Jehoshaphat. When he received word that enemies were advancing against Judah, he issued a call to prayer. "The people of Judah came together to seek help from the LORD; indeed, they came from every town in Judah to seek him" (2 Chronicles 20:4). The people cried out and worshiped God corporately. In response, God set ambushes against Judah's enemies, who were defeated, leaving all the plunder for the people of God.

When the early church gathered corporately to pray for Peter, who had been imprisoned for proclaiming the truth about Jesus's resurrection, God sent an angel to set him free (see Acts 12:5–10).

Where two or more are gathered...there is power.

Several years ago, I was sitting in the lobby of the Ritz Carlton in Atlanta, Georgia, surrounded by authors, editors, and agents attending the annual Christian Booksellers Association Convention. Suddenly, one of the authors announced that her wallet was missing. Clearly distraught, she and two others went off to retrace her steps. Immediately, God prompted me to pray. I stood up and said, "Let's join hands." Even though we were all in full-time Christian ministry, a crowded lobby in an elegant hotel didn't strike all of us as the right place for an impromptu prayer meeting. I don't think my colleagues could have been more shocked if I suggested we light a campfire and sing "Kumbaya."

Nevertheless, we joined hands, and I prayed a simple prayer: "Lord, you know where that wallet is. Our dear sister needs it back. We ask you to return it to her right now, in Jesus's name. Amen." No sooner had I said amen than her agent's phone rang. It was my agent calling to say, "Some total stranger just walked up to me and handed me your author's wallet." This, I promise you, is a true story!

Where two or more are gathered...there is power.

Some people say they are uncomfortable praying aloud. If you are one of them, ask yourself why. If you can stand around chatting with friends in public, then you can pray in public. If you can have a conversation with a human being, you can have a conversation with one or more human beings plus God. Prayer is just talking to God. It's the highest privilege we enjoy; why would we ever pass up the opportunity? Are you worried about embarrassing yourself or impressing someone else? Forget about trying to sound "spiritual"; just be yourself.

It's even possible to pray effectively when you're not even sure the other people know what you're talking about! That's what my friend Janet Barr discovered on a recent trip to Thailand, where she was teaching English as a second language. She recalls:

> On Sunday morning God reminded me, once again, that his ways are not our ways. We arrived at a small Thai church, added our shoes to the pile outside the door, and stepped into a simple sanctuary. After Dave preached and the service ended, the leader of the church announced that the visitors would be praying for those who had special needs.
>
> I was hesitant, but stood with the others at the front of the church, hoping that no one would come to me for prayer. Of course, that wasn't the case. Two ladies I had greeted earlier headed straight toward me. I felt helpless, but realized I was expected to pray. I started rather feebly, filled with regret that I couldn't understand their concerns. Then I remembered Timothy (a Thai with very limited English) was standing close by. I called him over and asked him to translate. As the women poured out their needs for physical healing, I started to pray. Timothy translated without hesitation. In moments, the power of the Lord became obvious, and we were praying together like

a well-oiled team. The women, now wreathed in smiles and relieved of their pain, at least for the moment, made their way out of the little church. Timothy and I just looked at each other in amazement. He later told our team leader he didn't know what had happened, but somehow he understood every word I prayed and was able to translate with little effort. Not a huge demonstration of power, I suppose, but enough to convince me that God was present at just the right time to bring healing into the lives of two simple Thai women who trusted him to work, in spite of the earthly limitations of language.

I love to pray with people! Almost every time I join hands with another follower of Jesus Christ and bow my head, I sense God's presence. I feel the warmth of his love and the depth of his concern. If you've not experienced the beauty of his presence "in the midst of these," you are missing out on one of the greatest joys of the Christian life.

Start praying with others. I didn't say exchange prayer requests. As you probably guessed, prayer requests are high on my list of pet peeves. What is the point of talking about what we need prayer for, when we could be using that valuable time praying? I don't get it. When it's time to pray, pray. Don't talk about praying. Don't build up to praying. Pray expecting God to show forth his power. Where two or more are gathered, God is in the midst!

⌒⌒

Dear heavenly Father, I thank you for the gift of corporate prayer. What a privilege to join with your children and bring our concerns directly into your throne room. Holy Spirit, help me to understand and overcome those things that have held me back from fully participating in corporate prayer. Give me freedom from self-consciousness and the ability to simply converse with God as I would with a loving parent. Thank you for the promise that where two or three are gathered in your name, you'll be right there. I want to make the most of that promise! Amen.

𝒜FFIRM

There's power in prayer when two or three are gathered.

𝒜PPLY

1. Do you think private prayer is more valuable than corporate prayer? Why or why not? Did today's reading change your perspective at all? In what way?

    _____

    _____

    _____

    _____

2. Do you find it difficult to pray in group settings? Why or why not?

_____

_____

_____

3. What are some things that might hinder our effectiveness in corporate prayer?

_____

_____

_____

4. Describe the most powerful experience you've ever had with corporate prayer.

_____

_____

_____

5. If you do not have a small group of Christians you regularly gather with for corporate prayer, make a list of some people you could invite to join you in praying together weekly. If you already have such a group, note some ways your prayer times might be more effective.

_____

_____

_____

$\mathcal{A}$CT

1. Plan a special time of corporate prayer.
2. Write out today's affirmation and scripture in your index-card notebook.
3. Write out your own prayer, expressing what God has shown you today about his mighty power.

_____

_____

_____

_____

Discover Soul-Rest

Come to me, all you who are weary and burdened,
and I will give you rest. Take my yoke upon you
and learn from me, for I am gentle and humble
in heart, and you will find rest for your souls.
For my yoke is easy and my burden is light.

MATTHEW 11:28–30

*M*y family has a tradition of watching *The Rosa Parks Story* each year on Martin Luther King Day. I'm sure most readers are familiar with her story, but just in case you're not, Rosa Parks was arrested when she refused to give up her seat to a white passenger on a public bus. An outcry ensued, followed by a bus boycott that, in many ways, marked the beginning of the American Civil Rights Movement.

During one scene in the movie, a teenager and an old man are waiting at a bus stop—not to board the bus, but to walk away from it in protest. The teen begins to complain about how tired he is, and the old man seems to agree with him, proclaiming that he, too, is weary. But then he explains to the young man why sacrifice is sometimes necessary, and then he adds, "These feet may be tired...but my soul is resting."

Few Western Christians appreciate the importance of Christ's invitation to find rest for our souls. We pursue leisure, but we rarely rest. We are a restless bunch, running here and there in relentless pursuit of one thing or another. We even run headlong into our Christian commitments, joining this committee and that, wearing ourselves out in the process.

Several years ago I heard a story about a woman I'll call Julie who was asked by a friend to housesit. The friend explained that her dog liked to chase Frisbees. Julie was excited about spending a relaxing weekend at her friend's beautiful beachfront home, and since she loved dogs, she thought it would be great to enjoy the dog's companionship. So the first night, she threw the Frisbee, and the dog leaped to retrieve it. The dog returned, dropped the Frisbee at Julie's feet, and anxiously insisted she throw it again. And again. And again. For over an hour, the dog frantically ran back and forth, leaping into the air, catching the Frisbee. He wouldn't stop! He couldn't stop! Julie was completely exasperated and thought, *I would love nothing more than to just sit and pet this dog. I had really been looking forward to spending time with him and just enjoying him…but he won't let me.*

I think God feels the same way about many Christians. Sometimes, I can almost hear him saying, *Stop leaping in the air, chasing Frisbees. Stop trying to impress me with all you can do. I'd much rather have you just sit right here with me. Let me enjoy your company, and I'll teach you how to enjoy mine.* We can't enjoy God's presence or hear God's voice when we're running at full speed, leaping into the air, only stopping at God's feet long enough to pant furiously, "Again!" Some of us have jumped higher and tried harder than anyone we know to show God, the world, and yes, maybe even ourselves, we can catch more Frisbees than anyone else in history.

No wonder many of us are exhausted. Here's the real problem: Frisbee chasing has absolutely nothing to do with the power of God; it's all about the power of the person doing the leaping. It's all about what we can, should, and will do for God...even if, by God, it kills us. Self-generated busyness doesn't unleash the power of God; in fact, it can hinder it. But it took me a long, long time to figure that out. I thought the key to experiencing God's power was leaping into the air and catching giant Frisbees with a single bound. Yes, indeed, I was the Queen of Frisbee Catching. I loved God with all my heart and desperately wanted to please him. It almost killed me. I have the medical bills to prove it.

One day, when I had reached the point of physical and emotional collapse, God led me to Psalm 23:

The LORD is my shepherd, I shall not be in want.
He makes me lie down in green pastures,
he leads me beside quiet waters,
he restores my soul.
He guides me in paths of righteousness
for his name's sake. (verses 1–3)

One phrase in particular caught my attention: "He makes me lie down." Some of us are so stubborn that the only way we'll get soul-rest is if God makes us lie down. I knew God was telling me, *Child, you need a good, long nap!* (And by the way, I'm not just talking about a physical nap here. I mean letting my soul rest securely in God's loving embrace.)

Any mother can tell you that naps are God's greatest gift to parents. We can all recall those days when our children were overtired and irritable. We knew that the best thing for our child was a nap, but that stubborn little one insisted, "Me not tired." But any parent who's been around that mountain before knows what happens when you take an overtired child out in public: humiliations galore. That napless bundle of terror reflects badly on your parenting skills. Everyone at the grocery store glares at you. You're just waiting for the checkout clerk to hand you the Bad Parent of the Year Award. So next time you do the smart thing: you make the child lie down and take a nap, even though he or she would rather be out running around. You love your child enough to say, "No more playing Frisbee; I'm making you lie down."

I don't know about you, but I've definitely made my heavenly Father look bad a time or two in the grocery store, the video store, and several other public places. If I live to be a hundred, I'll never forget the day I was pulling my hair out in a pizza parlor (neither my toddler nor I had had a nap on that particular day) when a woman came up to me with a puzzled expression and asked, "Aren't you Donna Partow?" *Forgive me, Father, for I haven't napped.*

When it reached the point where my Frisbee chasing for God left me so exhausted and irritable that God couldn't take me anywhere anymore, he made me lie down. Trust me on this one: a voluntary nap is far more pleasant than being sent to your room for an involuntary nap. God put my ministry on hold, and no matter how hard I tried to keep leaping in the air chasing Frisbees, no one would throw a Frisbee my way. God, in his severe mercy, made me lie down. Then he gently whispered, *Come to me, you who are weary and heavy laden, and I will give you rest for your soul.* He slowly began to teach me about the importance of having a soul at rest. Why not invite him to teach you as well? I promise that's a prayer request God is guaranteed to answer.

─────

Dear heavenly Father, I confess I've been chasing too many Frisbees. In my enthusiasm for experiencing God's power, I've gotten carried away with my own abilities—my own ability to leap in the air and put on a great show. Forgive me, Lord, for failing to heed your invitation to learn your unforced rhythm of grace. Forgive me, too, for those occasions when, out of sheer physical and emotional exhaustion, I've been a poor reflection of you, my loving heavenly Father. But I'm ready now. I'm ready to quit chasing Frisbees, and I'm ready to learn what it means to have a soul at rest. Teach me, Holy Spirit. Amen.

AFFIRM

I can find rest for my soul.

APPLY

1. Are you a Frisbee chaser? How so?

   _____

   _____

   _____

2. Do you agree that chasing Frisbees can hinder the power of God? Explain your answer.

_____

_____

_____

3. Describe a humorous or embarrassing incident—involving over-tired children—either your own or someone else's.

_____

_____

_____

4. Describe a time in your own life when God needed to make you lie down.

_____

_____

_____

5. What has God taught you about the importance of having a soul at rest?

_____

_____

_____

ACT

1. Take a nap.
2. Identify areas in your life where you may be chasing Frisbees—and stop.

3. Consider studying *Becoming the Woman I Want to Be: A 90-Day Journey to Renewing Spirit, Soul & Body* after completing this book. It outlines, step by step, the program God created for me to find rest for my soul. It has helped women around the world, from all walks of life, and I believe it will help you find rest for your soul as well.

4. Write out today's affirmation and scripture in your index-card notebook.

5. Write out your own prayer, expressing what God has shown you today about his mighty power.

_____

_____

_____

_____

Make the Most of the Sabbath

The Son of Man is Lord of the Sabbath.

MATTHEW 12:8

*F*inding rest for your soul isn't easy in this day and age. But apparently, it wasn't much easier in New Testament times, because the writer of Hebrews noted: "There remains, then, a Sabbath-rest for the people of God; for anyone who enters God's rest also rests from his own work, just as God did from his. Let us, therefore, make every effort to enter that rest" (4:9–11).

Did you catch that? We have to *make every effort* to enter rest. But the good news is, although it isn't easy to experience rest, it is possible. And it is well worth the effort. I emphasize effort, because rest is not going to drop down upon you apart from effort, and no one else can rest for you. It sounds contradictory, doesn't it, to make effort to enter rest. Yet, I've found that rest takes work. I have to carve out time if I want the rest I need. And I've found that the Sabbath is the best day to do your carving.

Actually, choosing to take Sundays off is a significant way to acknowledge our faith in God's power. It's a way of saying: *Heavenly Father, I believe your grace is more powerful than my work. I trust your love more than I trust my own efforts.* It's been said that when we work, we work. But when we pray, God works. Sunday is the perfect day to practice this truth by choosing *not* to work.

Not only do we rest from our usual work on Sundays, but my husband and I also try to make the day extra special. Sometimes, we get together with Christian friends after church. Other times, we just enjoy each other's company. My favorite Sundays are in the fall. That's when we put a pot of chili on the stove, cuddle up on the couch, and just chill. Sometimes we'll watch football. Praise the Lord, and go Eagles! (I believe the Philadelphia Eagles are going to see God's power at work and win the Super Bowl someday...very soon. You may consider that a word of prophecy!) Sometimes we'll simply relax and talk about nothin' in particular.

However, the highlight of our Sabbath rest is always our family communion time. I used to look forward to it all day, but I don't anymore. Now, I look forward to it *all week*. It is, without question, the most effective means we have discovered for experiencing God's power to transform our family.

This suggestion came to us from our dear friend Brother Paul McMahon. Brother Paul happens to be single, with no children of his own. He says this idea came to him as he was praying for our family. What a blessing to have such a dear member of my PIT crew.

Let me tell you a little about our service. Sometime around 7:00 p.m., I'll put soft praise music on. Then I'll set out crackers and pour grape juice into our beautiful clay cups, which I purchased while visiting The Potter's Place in Avanos, Turkey.[21] We gather in our prayer chapel and talk casually about the previous week. Then we'll usually read a Scripture passage and share a brief teaching. Next, one of us will read aloud prayers from one of our scripture/prayer books. We may share some thoughts about why we chose those prayers. Then we take turns confessing our sins and offering a word of encouragement to each person.

We have two simple rules: confess *your own* sins, and point out what everyone else did right. These rules apply to everyone and have proven 100 percent effective in ensuring that communion is always a powerful, spiritually uplifting time for everyone.

After a period of confession and encouragement—which lasts anywhere from fifteen minutes to an hour or more—we bow our heads and prepare ourselves for taking communion. Very often, one of us will have selected a special song to play for everyone to listen to while reflecting. Or we may listen to quiet praise music. When ready, each person walks to the small wooden chair to take the communion elements and then returns to his or her seat. At times, we have waited up to thirty minutes before everyone felt cleansed and ready to partake of communion. No one has ever rushed anyone else; we all sense that this is a sacred moment. The Bible says taking communion is serious business, and we take it seriously: "A man ought to examine himself before he eats of the bread and drinks of the cup. For anyone who eats and drinks without recognizing the body of the Lord eats and drinks judgment on himself" (1 Corinthians 11:28–29).

When everyone has the elements in hand, we recall the night Jesus was betrayed and how he ordained communion as a lasting remembrance. We also take a moment to pray for our persecuted brothers and sisters in other nations as God directs. Our prayer room is filled with items we've brought back from mission trips or that have been given to us by various missionary friends; they are around us as visual reminders that following Jesus often requires sacrifice, even as he sacrificed his life for us. We then partake.

Some evenings we'll linger awhile; other evenings we'll disband fairly quickly. Nothing is set in stone. One evening we remained in our prayer chapel for hours afterward, swept up in the beauty of God's powerful presence. More often then not, no one is in a hurry to leave the room.

Now that you're convinced my family could fit into future episodes of *Little House on the Prairie,* let me give you some background. In the months preceding our decision to have a weekly communion time, the level of conflict in our home had been escalating. My sixteen-year-old daughter, Leah, who had been homeschooled most of her life, had begun attending the local high school. I found her newfound interests and attitudes intolerable; she found my continuing efforts to control her every thought and action equally intolerable. A war of the wills was underway— and my teenager was winning. For some reason, all of our knock-down, drag-out fights occurred in what is now our prayer room. One day, I was sitting in there, and Leah said, "I don't know how you can stand to sit in the screaming room. All we ever do in here is fight."

The screaming room.

I was crushed to think my children would grow up remembering there was a room in our house devoted to screaming. That's when I decided to change the dynamic completely. I took almost everything out of that room and either threw it out, gave it away, or moved it elsewhere in the house. Then I moved every sacred object (crosses, Scripture-verse plaques, mission-trip artifacts, and so on) from elsewhere in the house into that one room. When I had re-created the room and spent an entire night praying aloud in it, anointing it with oil, and even sprinkling it with holy water, we celebrated with our first family communion.

Now that room is our favorite room. And guess what? Ever since we've instituted our weekly gatherings, the level of conflict in our family has plummeted. Yes, we still have our challenges, but there has definitely been a change in the atmosphere. And the perception of that room has turned 180 degrees—now it's the most peaceful room in the house. I believe the peace we are fostering in that room is permeating the rest of the house. Peace has a powerful way of spreading.

Last Sunday, our family communion time lasted two hours and was filled with laughter. It was our first time together after being apart for several Sundays—first Tara was away, then Leah and I were on a mission trip. It was truly a celebration—and the dog forgave us all for abandoning her! Each Sunday is unique but special in its own way. I'm thankful to God, and our dear Brother Paul, for the precious gift of family communion. I commend it to your family and pray it will be a blessed time of entering his rest and experiencing God's power to heal and strengthen your family.

Note: if you believe only a priest or pastor can conduct a communion service, I can certainly respect your position. I encourage you to honor your own convictions and refrain from the bread and the cup. You may, however, want to incorporate all other elements in a family Sabbath celebration. Perhaps you could invite your priest or pastor to join you some Sunday and conduct communion for you.

⁓

Dear heavenly Father, thank you for the gift of Sabbath, and for the even greater gift of loved ones. Holy Spirit, teach me how to find balance in the area of rest. I don't want to come under the law and go overboard; but neither do I want to miss out on the blessings of the Sabbath. I want to experience the power of God that's available to those who trust you enough to rest from their labors one day a week. Please also help me to discern the best way for me [and my family] to make the most of a weekly Sabbath celebration. I am open to your leading and direction. Amen.

AFFIRM

I acknowledge my faith in God's power by choosing to take a day off each week.

APPLY

1. How do you currently honor the Sabbath?

   _____

   _____

   _____

2. What is your reaction to the suggestion for family communion?

   _____

   _____

   _____

3. What components of a family communion service might you incorporate into your life?

_____

_____

_____

4. Describe your plans for making the Sabbath into a day for rest.

_____

_____

_____

5. How can you get your family involved in the process?

_____

_____

_____

ACT

1. Consider starting a tradition of family communion. If that seems unsuitable, think of other ways to make the Sabbath special.
2. If you do not currently have a prayer room in your house, consider creating one.
3. Write out today's affirmation and scripture in your index-card notebook.

4. Write out your own prayer, expressing what God has shown you today about his mighty power.

_____

_____

_____

_____

Trust God's Promises

*His divine power has given us everything we
need for life and godliness through our knowledge
of him who called us by his own glory and goodness.
Through these he has given us his very great and
precious promises, so that through them you may
participate in the divine nature and escape the
corruption in the world caused by evil desires.*

2 PETER 1:3–4

I've battled many formidable foes in my lifetime, from drug addiction to witch doctors. But my war of a lifetime is a war I wage within. The enemy? Insecurity. Sometimes I think I'm the only one, but recently, one of my insightful counselors, Karen Lusher, sent me the following e-mail in response to my request for her input on this book:

I'm convinced that insecurity is a huge stumbling block in the body of Christ today. The Lord has been teaching me that I have one title alone: I'm God's child. If I experience his love by focusing on him day by day, rejection issues will disappear. My

Father, who is the creator of all there is, tells me I'm cherished. As I hear him and receive his love, my joy is full. Then if a person rejects me or does not like me, instead of feeling rejection, it is almost laughable, for the One at the top thinks I'm wonderful. Because I'm in Jesus. As I keep receiving that love, it starts to pour out of me to others.

Personal insecurities are a giant energy drain. They sap the power of God from our lives, because they cause our prayers and even our ministries to be motivated by fear, jealousy, and personal ambition rather than by the love of God. We're held captive by "the corruption in the world caused by evil desires" (2 Peter 1:4). Wrong motives taint even the good things we attempt to do *for God*. And since every prayer we pray from wrong motives goes unanswered, our efforts yield no fruit. Frustration and emotional exhaustion soon follow. We experience the painful truth of Scripture: "You have planted much, but have harvested little" (Haggai 1:6).

The first time I read that passage, I wept for hours. It described my predicament exactly. As an insecure person, I had become caught in a vicious cycle. I wanted to serve God, if for no other reason than to justify my place in his family. But because insecurity tainted my motives, my service was ineffective and unproductive. In fact, some efforts were downright destructive.

Perhaps you can relate. Insecure people don't think they are worthy of God's blessings simply because they are his beloved children; insecure people believe they have to earn them. Insecure people desperately seek the approval they think they need, instead of simply standing on God's promise that he has *already* freely given them everything they need to live a God-infused life. God's divine power is the only possible source of authentic power, and that divine power can never be earned. We don't experience God's power by our own self-effort; it flows from *his goodness*.

It's not accessed by formulas or programs; God's divine power is available to us *through trust in his promises.*

When we think about it, it's amazing how many destructive things people do because of personal insecurities. Of course, all human beings are a complex mix of motives, but how many people have premarital sex or extramarital affairs just because they're insecure and need to feel loved? How many people become slaves to their careers, alienating their families and jeopardizing their health, because they're insecure and need to feel important? How many people do drugs, either to medicate the pain of their insecurities or to make themselves feel invincible, if only while the high lasts? How many people live consumed by selfishness and greed, because they are insecure and fear that if they don't care for themselves, no one else will either?

Think about these questions: How many women launch speaking ministries, and how many men build megachurches because they are insecure and desperate for applause? (I'd give you my opinion, but it would get me into too much trouble!) How many people volunteer at church because they are insecure and desperately lonely? James is talking to *church members* when he says: "What causes fights and quarrels among you? Don't they come from your desires that battle within you?" (James 4:1).

Do you want to know what gets me in trouble *every time?* Do you want to know the root of 99 percent of my problems? My fears and insecurities drive me to take matters into my own hands. Yes, even in matters of ministry. If you ever want a good laugh, come hang out with me sometime when I'm trying to figure everything out. *Why, God, why? When, God, when? How much longer? Did you really say...?* Actually, it's not really all that funny. It's just a sad, sorry sight. The question I should be asking is, *When, Donna, when? When will you simply* believe *what God has promised?*

On that day, and not one day before, I'll begin to "participate in the divine nature" and "escape the corruption in the world" (2 Peter 1:4). On that day, I'll begin to enjoy the benefits of God's divine power. When I don't stand on God's promises, I'm in emotional anguish; and fear, rather than faith, motivates everything I do. Unfortunately, "everything that does not come from faith is sin" (Romans 14:23).

Speaking of promises, if you ever visit my house, beware of the most powerful force known to Partowdom: the pinky promise. Let me explain. Our daughter Tara never forgets a promise, especially if it is for ice cream or some other treat. Tara learned very early that parents sometimes try to weasel their way out of promises by dreaming up—*oops, I mean pointing out*—little-known provisos. To protect herself against disappointment, Tara discovered the power of the pinky finger. If we try to back out of a promise we made to her, she simply lifts up that sweet little finger, and we snap to attention.

Unlike us, God isn't looking for ways to weasel out of keeping his promises. In fact, the opposite is true: he's searching for people with enough spunk to lift their pinky finger, declaring, *I expect you to be true to your Word.* He welcomes it. He delights in it.

Our lives become conduits for the power of God when we trust God to do what he has promised to do. It's God's job to keep his promises, and it's impossible for him to fail. He is on task 24/7: "He who watches over you will not slumber" (Psalm 121:3). What's our job? To make every effort to become, first and foremost, people of *faith.* "Add to your faith" (2 Peter 1:5). Our job is to believe God will be true to his Word. That's why we're called believers. When God sees someone who *believes his promises,* he will move heaven and earth to reward that person's faith.

That's what he did for Abraham. Because Abraham "believed God, and it was credited to him as righteousness"—a fact that is mentioned in Genesis 15:6, Romans 4:3, Galatians 3:6, and James 2:23. We're told that "he did not waver through unbelief regarding the promise of God, but was strengthened in his faith and gave glory to God, being fully persuaded that God had power to do what he had promised" (Romans 4:20–21). Wow! *Fully persuaded that God had power to do what he had promised.* Such confidence in God leaves zero room for insecurity. Isn't that how you want to live each day of your life? I know it's what I long for.

When Abraham was seventy-five, God appeared to him, promising to make him a great nation (see Genesis 12:1–3). Twenty-four years later, Abraham still believed God would keep his promise to make him the father of many nations (see Genesis 17:5) even though Abraham hadn't fathered his first child. I don't know about you, but if after twenty-four *hours* God hasn't fulfilled something I believe he has spoken, my faith starts getting a bit shaky. Can you imagine holding on for twenty-four *years* for God to fulfill his promise to you? Maybe you can. Maybe it's been more than twenty-four years. Or maybe the difficulty is not the amount of time you've been waiting but the obstacles you are facing. Maybe you're like John.

John's wife became pregnant by another man, but John loved the baby with all his heart anyway. When the baby was less than a year old, John's wife walked out on all of her responsibilities, so John raised the child alone for the next three years. Then one day his wife returned and demanded full custody along with a paternity test that proved John wasn't the father. But John believed God, the ultimate Judge, would rule in his favor. When the family went into the courtroom, the judge was initially extremely antagonistic, grilling John with tough questions. Right in the middle of questioning, John bowed his head and started praying. Silence fell over the courtroom. The judge immediately changed his attitude, granting John joint custody. That was several years ago. Today, John has his daughter more than 90 percent of the time.

God's promises bring us face to face with one of the most difficult choices every Christian must make: *Will I believe God's promises…or will*

I take matters into my own hands? "They that wait upon the LORD shall renew their strength" (Isaiah 40:31, KJV) while those who take matters into their own hands shall exhaust themselves and everyone around them.

Maybe you are at that crossroads at this very moment. Believe God's promise: "Now to him who is able to do immeasurably more than all we ask or imagine, according to his power that is at work within us, to him be glory in the church and in Christ Jesus throughout all generations, for ever and ever! Amen" (Ephesians 3:20–21).

Dear heavenly Father, thank you for being a God who keeps his promises. I long to become your friend—someone who believes you keep your promises. Forgive me for those occasions when I've had more trust in people than in you. Forgive me for the times I've doubted you. Lord, I want to discover what it truly means to have power-packed faith—I want to believe you'll do the miraculous in and through my life. I believe you will keep your promises to me. Amen.

AFFIRM

I believe God keeps his promises.

APPLY

1. Do you believe God is eager to keep his promises? Why or why not?

   _____

   _____

   _____

2. Recall a time in your life when you had enough spunk to lift up your pinky finger and say, *God, I know you are going to keep this promise.* What were the results?

   _____

   _____

   _____

3. Can you think of a situation in your life right now that requires you to believe God will keep his promises, or else? What specific promises are you looking to God to keep?

   _____

   _____

   _____

4. Describe a time when God kept his promise in a powerful way.

   _____

   _____

   _____

5. What would it take for you to become a friend of God's?

_____

_____

_____

$\mathcal{A}$CT

1. Search the Bible, marking any of God's promises that speak to you in your current situation. Now reach up that pinky finger!
2. Write out today's affirmation and scripture in your index-card notebook.
3. Write out your own prayer, expressing what God has shown you today about his mighty power.

_____

_____

_____

_____

'Behave as God's Child

*Be wise in the way you act toward outsiders; make
the most of every opportunity. Let your conversation
be always full of grace, seasoned with salt, so that
you may know how to answer everyone.*

Colossians 4:5–6

*M*arie almost always flies first class. That wouldn't be so remarkable except that she never buys a first-class ticket. For some
"mysterious" reason, either the gate agent or a flight attendant invariably
moves Marie to first class.

Honestly, it used to annoy me. No one ever did me any favors. Quite
the opposite. People seemed eager to make my life more difficult. I
couldn't figure out why God kept making arrangements for half the
planet to fall all over themselves to give Marie preferential treatment, but
not me. In short, I was jealous.

So I started watching Marie closely, secretly hoping to find some fault
in her. Then I could yell, "See, she ain't all that great!" thereby dragging
her down to my level so, in some sick way, I could feel better about

myself. I know you never do anything like that, but there you have the awful truth about me. Anyway, there were a few things I noticed about Marie that gave me pause to adjust my attitude.

First, she never says anything negative about anything—ever. It's her firm policy. If you gossip or criticize around Marie, she will gently lift her hand up and wave off your comment, smiling graciously the whole time. She does this in such an adorable, sweet-spirited way that it's impossible to be offended. If she doesn't have something nice to say, she keeps her mouth shut. If she has a problem with someone, she doesn't say a word to anyone. Except God. She tells him all about everything and trusts him to handle her concerns. I used to think Marie had taken her positive attitude to the extreme. I mean, hey, we've got to live in the real world, right? But since Marie's approach to life works so incredibly well, I began to think maybe she was onto something.

Marie is also one of the most avid Bible students I've ever met. Her day starts at 5:00 a.m., and she spends at least two or three hours studying God's Word for the two Bible classes she teaches each week. She has memorized a truckload of Bible verses, and they seem to just flow out of her mouth effortlessly.

Not only that, Marie fasts at least one day a week, and frequently fasts for seven, ten, and even forty-day periods so she can devote herself to prayer. She's especially committed to praying for her family. Her husband and two grown sons with both their wives are all serving in full-time ministry; one son preaches in massive outdoor campaigns overseas. As a result of her frequent fasting, not only is Marie's family powerfully blessed, and not only is she a mighty prayer warrior—she doesn't carry an ounce of excess weight. Although she's nearly sixty years old, you'd never guess it by her physique. She's more fit than most teenagers. In fact, she saves money by shopping in the teen department. Marie says they have better prices on the latest fashions.

Marie always looks sensational. She even looked sensational one day when I bumped into her at Jamba Juice. She was wearing jeans and a casual shirt, yet Marie still looked terrific. Marie still looked first class.

That's when it hit me. *Marie gets bumped to first class because it's obvious she belongs in first class.* She exudes the fruit of the Spirit. She conducts herself like a child of the King, and people treat her accordingly. There's just *something about Marie*! The power of God has transformed her from the inside out, and that transformation is so dramatic, so appealing, people *want* to treat her well.

When we act right, people will almost always treat us right. Not always, of course. Sometimes Christians are persecuted for their faith. This is especially true outside the Western world. Here in the West, few Christians are persecuted for their faith. However, many are treated badly because they behave badly.

When we choose to conduct ourselves as God's children, whether others are treating us well or poorly, we stand out, allowing us to testify to the transforming power of God in our lives. When we allow the Holy Spirit to flow through us, our lives overflow with love, joy, peace, patience, kindness, goodness, faithfulness, gentleness, and self-control, *no matter what happens*. The world is filled with nasty, demanding people; someone who refuses to behave badly will get people's attention.

Take the case of Paul and Silas in Acts 16. They were stripped naked and "severely flogged" (verse 23), then thrown into prison, where they were locked in a cell with their feet in stocks. It's hard to imagine worse conditions. Nevertheless, Paul and Silas chose to conduct themselves as God's children. Rather than complaining, they were "praying and singing hymns to God" (verse 25). No wonder "the other prisoners were listening to them" (verse 25). However, other people weren't the only ones who took notice. God got involved and did much more than upgrade their seats! He sent an earthquake that shook the very foundations of the prison and caused the prison doors to fly open. Not only were Paul and Silas released from their chains, but the Bible tells us "everybody's chains came loose" (verse 26).

Wow. That speaks powerfully, doesn't it? No matter where you are right now, no matter how trapped or hopeless you might feel, if you choose to release the power of God within, God will unleash his power into your circumstances. A faith real enough and powerful enough to enable us to sing in our own prison cell is a faith that's real enough and powerful enough to impact everyone around us. And the converse is also true. If our faith is *not* setting people around us free from their chains, let's examine ourselves and ask God how we can become more effective vessels of his power.

The impact of Paul and Silas's faith doesn't end with the release of their fellow prisoners. It goes straight to the top of the prison authorities. The warden himself fell on his knees, asking Paul and Silas, "Sirs, what must I do to be saved?" (verse 30). Paul and Silas then "spoke the word of the Lord to him and to all the others in his house" and "he and all his family were baptized" (verses 32–33). But something significant happened between those two events—"the jailer took them and washed their wounds" (verse 33). He changed the way he treated them; he upgraded them from prisoners to houseguests; he "brought them into his house and set a meal before them" (verse 34).

Let me say that I have a long way to go in this area—that's the bad news. The good news is that I no longer beat myself up over that fact as I did in the past. In those awful days, I would have taken out my so-called prayer journal and written page after page of self-hate-filled commentary about what a pathetic loser I was and how God himself probably didn't like me. More recently, I've been praying that God would unleash his power *in* me and change me. I'm not even close to where Marie is, but I did have one interesting experience worth sharing.

I had been thinking a lot about Marie's first-class upgrades, because I fly all the time, and unlike Marie, I usually end up with the middle seat in the last row. I kid you not. I have lost track of the number of times I've been seated in the last row. It used to make me crazy. I'd sit there alternately sulking and complaining at the top of my lungs. Yet I couldn't figure out why no one ever upgraded me to first class. Hmm.

Anyway, there I sat one day awaiting my flight, thinking about Marie. Suddenly, I heard a man shouting at the gate agent. He was right in her face, behaving belligerently. Although I probably should have asked myself WWJD, instead I wondered, *What would Marie do?* I started praying, then walked over and gently began rubbing the man's back in a motherly, "It's going to be okay" sort of way. He looked at me like, *Who on earth are you?* but I just smiled, not saying a word. The man was caught off guard. My gentleness was such a dramatic contrast to the mayhem he was creating that he began to calm down. When he finally came up for air, I asked in a voice so low it bordered on a whisper, "Can I help you somehow?"

He explained his predicament: he and his small child were not seated together, and the gate agent was unable to reassign them. I assured him we would have no difficulty finding someone to switch seats and added that I would speak to every passenger on the flight if that's what it took. I boarded the plane along with the young man and his son and helped them find two seats together, then sat down. A few minutes later, the gate agent came onboard and informed me that she wanted to speak with me. She had upgraded me to first class!

Whether you're in a prison cell or an airport terminal, the Holy Spirit can give you the power within to behave as God's child. And as an added bonus, you may just get an upgrade in your circumstance.

*Dear heavenly Father, thank you for the power of the Holy
Spirit, who can enable me to conduct myself in a way
worthy of the gospel at all times. Forgive me for those times
I've failed to access the grace I needed to behave as your
child in the midst of trying circumstances. I sincerely desire
to be a positive reflection on you and your kingdom. Amen.*

AFFIRM

I can behave as God's child.

APPLY

1. What is your reaction to the story about Marie?

_____

_____

_____

2. What are some things you noticed about Marie's lifestyle that would incline people to show her favorable treatment?

_____

_____

_____

3. How similar is your lifestyle to Marie's? How often are you able to tap into "the grace to behave as his child" in the midst of trying circumstances?

_____

_____

_____

4. Describe your most powerful experience when the Holy Spirit gave you grace to behave as God's child in a difficult situation.

_____

_____

_____

5. Can you think of some circumstances you might routinely encounter (traffic jams, waiting in lines, and so on) when you might be tempted *not* to behave as God's child? How can you prepare yourself to handle such circumstances with more grace?

_____

_____

_____

ACT

1. Make a conscious decision to behave as God's child in the next difficult situation you encounter.
2. Write out today's affirmation and scripture in your index-card notebook.
3. Write out your own prayer, expressing what God has shown you today about his mighty power.

_____

_____

_____

_____

Cultivate Power Within and Power Upon

*To him who is able to do immeasurably more
than all we ask or imagine, according to his
power that is at work within us, to him be
glory in the church and in Christ Jesus throughout
all generations, for ever and ever! Amen.*

EPHESIANS 3:20–21

*I*t's been said that there's nothing worse than a small character in a big assignment. Such people can put on an impressive display, at least for a season, but eventually their lack of integrity leads to their collapse. Unfortunately, it may also lead to the collapse of entire families, churches, and ministries. These people are what T. S. Eliot called "The Hollow Men."

However, after twenty-five years in the church, I may have discovered something even worse: a big character refusing to tackle any assignment. While a solid Christian sitting in the pew will never make tabloid headlines in the same way a fallen Christian in the pulpit will, it's no less a tragedy when Christians who love God fail to exercise their spiritual gifts. While these believers may not be obviously destructive, their failure to produce a harvest for the kingdom robs the world daily. While their immediate circle of family and friends benefit from the fruit in these believers' lives, the world at large does not.

The statement of faith of many churches includes an assertion that the Holy Spirit's primary work is transforming our character, empowering us to lead godly lives. That is certainly true, but it is not the entire truth. Yes, we have been given the Holy Spirit to produce the peaceable fruit of righteousness. But he also empowers us for the work of the kingdom. God wants to pour his Spirit on us so that we can do the greater works Jesus spoke about (see John 14:12). He gave us spiritual gifts so we could exercise them for the benefit of others: "In the church God has appointed first of all apostles, second prophets, third teachers, then workers of miracles, also those having gifts of healing, those able to help others, those with gifts of administration, and those speaking in different kinds of tongues" (1 Corinthians 12:28).

In addition to using our gifts within the church, we should extend our service outside the church walls. Jesus said we are the light of the world and that our light shouldn't be hidden behind closed doors. It's good to share all that we are and all that we have with our Christian friends. But it's not enough. That's what God told Isaiah: "It is too small a thing for you to be my servant to restore the tribes of Jacob and bring back those of Israel I have kept. I will also make you a light for the Gentiles, that you may bring my salvation to the ends of the earth" (Isaiah 49:6). He didn't say it was a bad thing, just too small a thing. It's certainly not bad for Christians to minister to one another. It's just too small a thing. We have a big God with a big heart for a big world—almost seven billion people, many of whom have no opportunity to see "Jesus with skin on."

The apostle Paul urged Roman believers to offer their lives as "living sacrifices" to God (12:1). Then, in the next paragraph he clarified his meaning: "We have different gifts, according to the grace given us. If a man's gift is prophesying, let him use it in proportion to his faith. If it is serving, let him serve; if it is teaching, let him teach; if it is encouraging, let him encourage; if it is contributing to the needs of others, let him give generously; if it is leadership, let him govern diligently; if it is showing mercy, let him do it cheerfully" (12:6–8).

In the twelfth chapter of Romans, Paul told them, and us, to "share with God's people who are in need" (verse 13), but that must include God's people all over the world, not just in our local church. The admonitions to "bless those who persecute you" and "overcome evil with good" should make it obvious that Paul assumes our living sacrifice will extend beyond our family of faith (verses 14, 21).

A power-packed Christian life includes the unleashing power of the Holy Spirit within us, producing the fruit of righteousness in us. It also includes the Holy Spirit upon us, yielding a harvest of souls for the kingdom. We need the power of God for both, and we'll never fully experience the power of God in our lives until we give equal attention to both areas.

God's power is unleashed wherever Christians are open to both power within and power upon. I've spoken in churches where women had their heads covered and in churches where people were doing cartwheels down the aisle until midnight. I've sung hymns with Presbyterians and swayed to a gospel-jazz-soul trio with Church of God women. I've taken communion with Catholics and Episcopalians; and I've been swept up into mighty free-flowing moves of the Holy Spirit with charismatics. I've ministered to the homeless, alcoholics, drug addicts, and battered women alongside the Salvation Army. I've prayed with a Muslim convert in a cave in Turkey and with converts from animism in the jungles of Papua New Guinea. I have been privileged to speak at the CIA headquarters on two separate occasions, and I have shared the gospel on crowded street corners in South America.

I've ministered to a variety of denominations, including Anglican, Assemblies of God, Baptist, Bible, Brethren, Calvary Chapel, Catholic, independent charismatic, Church of God, Episcopalian, Evangelical Free, Lutheran, Lutheran Brethren, Mennonite, Methodist, Nazarene, Presbyterian (OPC, PCA, PCUSA, you name it!), Reformed, Salvation Army, Vineyard, Wesleyan, and the Worldwide Church of God. I've learned something from Christians in *every one* of these churches.

This is a generalization, but I've observed that churches tend to focus on *either* spiritual fruit or spiritual gifts. Churches that emphasize spiritual fruit but don't exercise spiritual gifts stunt the work of God. Often they struggle against tradition for tradition's sake, ritualism, and a dry, dusty spirituality. Their congregations tend to be small with a noticeable absence of younger people and few, if any, new believers. In recent years, half of all American churches did not add one new member through conversion growth. Eighty-five percent of American churches are declining or at a plateau. Of the 15 percent that are growing, most are doing so at the expense of other churches. Here's the most shocking statistic: five hundred billion dollars have been spent on church growth in the United States in the last fifteen years with no appreciable impact on our culture. Meanwhile, church attendance among all Protestant denominations *decreased* 9.5 percent in the last ten years, even though the population *increased* by 11.4 percent.[22]

Churches that encourage their members to exercise their spiritual gifts are growing at a much faster rate than those who do not. However, because these churches don't always give equal attention to spiritual fruit, they can stunt the character of their congregants and put the long-term future of God's work in jeopardy. Although bursting at the seams with an influx of younger people and new believers, they sometimes struggle against carnality and controversy.

Our best hope for powerful, effective churches is through a combination of spiritual fruit and gifts—power within and power upon. Such an approach will yield a balanced congregation with a wide variety of members who are vessels of God's power. Power within plus power upon work together to form more than one plus one. When power within and power upon combine, the results are exponential!

Think of Billy Graham. He has preached to over 210 million people in 185 countries and territories.[23] Not only has he traveled around the world exercising his spiritual gift of evangelism, but no allegation against his character has ever been able to stand. He has experienced *power upon* his ministry to lead millions to Christ and *power within* to conduct that ministry with integrity since 1939, and this powerful combination has sustained him as a vessel of God's power.

The same combination has worked for Ellen, a pastor's wife of an ordinary-sized congregation in an ordinary American suburb. But there's nothing ordinary about this woman. Not only does her life exude a vibrant faith characterized by love, joy, and peace, but she also exercises the power of the Holy Spirit everywhere she goes. I've seen her wander up to a group of teenagers in a public park, strike up a conversation, open up her Bible, and start teaching. She leads a women's Sunday-school class and frequently joins the worship team, but she also evangelizes in grocery stores, lays hands on the sick in parking lots (and they get healed!), receives prophetic insight about strangers that leaves them speechless—and heading for church on Sunday.

The Bible's Stephen also serves as a powerful example of power within and power upon. In the sixth chapter of Acts, the twelve disciples decide to choose seven men to help meet the practical needs of widows in the church. They wanted to choose responsible men who were "known to be full of the Spirit and wisdom" (verse 3), so "they chose Stephen, a man full of faith and of the Holy Spirit" (verse 5). Clearly, he was experiencing power within.

But there was more to Stephen than godly character. "Now Stephen, a man full of God's grace and power, did great wonders and miraculous signs among the people" (verse 8). That's power upon. However, power within and power upon did not exempt Stephen from hardship. In his case, the combination invited it. He was dragged before the Sanhedrin, and even though everyone in the room "saw that his face was like the face of an angel" (verse 15), even though he had profound understanding of the Old Testament Scriptures and presented the gospel with compelling authority, they still stoned him to death. Yet even as they were killing him, the power of God within Stephen enabled him to forgive his executioners.

The lesson from Stephen is this: let's not deceive ourselves into thinking power-packed faith is our ticket to an easy life. If your goal is comfort and convenience, you're reading the wrong book! The purpose of becoming a vessel of God's power is not to benefit *ourselves;* it's to advance God's kingdom upon the earth. In life and in death, that's exactly what Stephen did. It's what God wants us to do as well.

⁓

Dear heavenly Father, thank you for the incredible gift of the Holy Spirit. I recognize my need for the work of the Spirit within me to cultivate the fruit of the Spirit in my life. I want to be a person characterized by love, joy, peace, patience, kindness, goodness, faithfulness, gentleness, and self-control. But I also want power upon my life, energizing my spiritual gifts and enabling me to do greater works than I've ever dared to dream possible. I want my life to count for your kingdom, and I know that will only happen as I demonstrate your power to a watching world. Holy Spirit, make me a power-packed vessel you can use! Amen.

AFFIRM

The Holy Spirit gives me both power within and power upon my life.

APPLY

1. Describe how you would be if you cultivated power within to such an extent that your character was transformed. What does the ideal *you* look like on the inside?

   _____

   _____

   _____

2. Do you place more importance on power within (spiritual fruit) or power upon (spiritual gifts)? Is one a higher priority in your personal walk with God? Which one, and why?

   _____

   _____

   _____

3. Does your church emphasize gifts or fruit, or is there a healthy pursuit of both? What has been the outcome?

_____

_____

_____

4. Describe someone you know who demonstrates both power within and power upon.

_____

_____

_____

5. What are some practical steps you can take to cultivate both power within and power upon?

_____

_____

_____

*A*CT

1. Take a spiritual gifts test. I recommend "Discover Your God-Given Gifts" by Don and Katie Fortune (www.heart2 heart.org).
2. Write out today's affirmation and scripture in your index-card notebook.

3. Write out your own prayer, expressing what God has shown you today about his mighty power.

_____

_____

_____

_____

'Find Power in Weakness

But [the Lord] said to me, "My grace is sufficient for
you, for my power is made perfect in weakness."
Therefore I will boast all the more gladly about my
weaknesses, so that Christ's power may rest on me.

2 CORINTHIANS 12:9

Two years ago, I visited the Embera Indian tribe in Central America. (They portrayed the Waodani in the film *End of the Spear.*) On the way to their village, our canoe repeatedly grounded in the middle of the depleted river, and our guides had to climb out to push us through the mud. When we arrived at the village, the Embera informed us that they were facing dire circumstances due to the lack of rain. These tribal people live on fish and rely on the trading business they conduct with river travelers. No rain meant no river, no fish, no income. Their situation couldn't get much worse than that.

I was traveling with a group of Christians, so we began singing praises to God and declaring our confidence that if Jesus could calm a storm, he could certainly send one too. Although the sky was blue, with not a cloud in sight, we prayed with assurance that God would send rain. Within minutes, we heard thunder in the distance and were suddenly in the middle of a torrential downpour that lasted all day and through the night. Talk about the power of God!

You may have noticed that many of my examples of times when I've experienced God's power occur outside the United States. Maybe that troubles you; I know it troubled me, so much so that I sat down with one of my most trusted, insightful counselors to discuss the matter. "What this book needs," I lamented, "are examples of God's power in our ordinary, everyday lives." We both agreed I could sell a truckload of books if I could uncover the secret to unlocking God's power in such a setting, because that's what almost everyone wants. I've spent most of the past year writing this book with that goal in mind. Day after day I prayed, *Lord, show me the secret, show me the key, reveal to me what the missing ingredient is in so many of our lives.*

Deep inside I think I wanted to give people what I thought they wanted: a strategy that would enable us to go on living much as we've always lived and just *add* God's power to it. When my kids and I go to Jamba Juice to order our favorite fruit shakes, we get to pick our favorite "add in" or "booster." We can add a protein boost, an immunity boost, or even an energy boost. Wouldn't it be fabulous if we could have that option when it comes to our spiritual lives? We could say, *Okay, God, I'd like to order one comfortable, suburban American life—with a supernatural boost.*

Unfortunately, God's power doesn't operate that way. It's not something we can simply add to our lives whenever it suits us. Whether we like it or not, the Bible plainly demonstrates—from start to finish—that God's power only manifests when two conditions are met: we genuinely need it and, more important, *we humble ourselves enough to admit we need it.* His power is strong when we are weak. Period.

Too many of us have organized our lives so we don't need God's power, and then we wonder why we never experience it. I'll be the first to admit:

guilty, guilty, guilty! Even our prayers boil down to: *Dear God, please set up my life so perfectly that I don't need you or anyone else.* Then we scratch our heads when others see God moving in a dramatic fashion, even though we never do. Most Americans are proud of their self-sufficiency. Our theme song is "I Did It My Way" with emphasis on the I. *I, me, my.* We leave no room for God. However, throughout Scripture, throughout history, throughout the world today, God's power is given to those who recognize their need for it.

Two of the most inspiring books I've read lately are *Always Enough* by Rolland and Heidi Baker and *The Heavenly Man* by Brother Yun. Both are filled with stories of miracles. Is that because the Bakers and Brother Yun are God's favorite children? Does God like them more than he likes other Christians, so he answers their prayers and ignores ours? No. These saints experience daily miracles because they *need* daily miracles, and they know it. Heidi Baker cares for two thousand orphans in Mozambique; she and her husband have been used by God to found more than five thousand churches in the midst of the most difficult circumstances imaginable: flooding, famine, war—you name it. Brother Yun suffered unspeakable torture in Chinese prisons and now works on behalf of the persecuted church worldwide. None of these believers could survive one day without God's power, and they readily admit it.

How long could you survive without God's direct intervention in your life? I'm going to make a very bold statement: the longer you can survive without God's direct intervention, the less likely you are to experience God's power. If you can say of your life, "If all goes as planned, I should be okay," don't expect to see a mighty move of God. It's time to get real here, friends. Many of us have inadvertently power-proofed our lives, and we don't even know it.

Until we recognize our desperate need for God's intervention, he will watch quietly, patiently waiting until we get it through our thick skulls that he wants to do so much more in and through our lives. If you want to experience God's power, if you want to see a miracle with your own eyes, you've got to put yourself in a place where you can honestly say, "If God doesn't show up, I'm in a whole heap of trouble." One of my favorite preachers is Jackson Senyonga, pastor of the sixty-thousand-member Christian Life Ministries Church in Kampala, Uganda. He often says, "God rides on the wings of desperation." It's when we're at our most desperate that God works most powerfully.

As radical as this may sound, I encourage you to deliberately put yourself in a place where you are desperate for God. Frankly, few things will do that as quickly and effectively as a short-term mission trip, although anything that takes you out of your comfort zone will work. Nothing can drive you to your knees quicker than unfamiliar surroundings. Suddenly, your self-sufficiency crumbles, and you come face to face with your need. We'll never understand and enter into all God wants us to experience until we lay aside our self-sufficiency.

Three gospel writers—Matthew, Mark, and Luke—thought Jesus's remarks about the rich man and the camel were important enough to include in their eyewitness accounts of Jesus's life. (By the way, if you live in the United States, you *are* rich, whether you think so or not. Three billion people currently live on less than two dollars per day.[24] One and one-half billion live on less than a dollar a day. Even the poorest person in the United States lives better than most people on earth. So this verse *is addressed to you*, not the even-richer person down the street.) Jesus said, "It is easier for a camel to go through the eye of a needle than for a rich man to enter the kingdom of God" (Matthew 19:24; Mark 10:25; Luke 18:25). The obvious interpretation is that Jesus is talking about salvation, but more broadly, he's talking about our ability to benefit from all that the king's dominion has to offer; all that it means to be rightful heirs, sons and daughters of the King.

The Eye of the Needle was actually a low entry gate through the wall that surrounded the city of Jerusalem. Camels *could* get through this gate, but *only if* they first let their owners unload them so they could crawl through on their knees. Picture the scene. These camels were coming into the city, loaded with riches to sell. In a sense, they were carrying their paycheck on their backs. They were loaded down with everything that enabled them to be self-sufficient.

Think about this too: that load of stuff may have been valuable, it may have been their ticket to financial security, but it was also *a burden to bear.* Sound familiar? It was an act of compassion when the owners untied their camels' loads, because otherwise the camels would struggle in vain and *never* be able to enter into the city. God loves us so much that he comes along and unties our ropes and let's our baggage fall to the ground as well. Then and only then will you experience his power.

I think that's what Jesus is talking about. We have to humble ourselves and release all those things we're relying on, all those things that enable us to make it on our own. At the time Jesus lived, religious people believed material wealth was your reward for being such a good, upstanding person. That's why everyone who heard Jesus say this was astonished and said, "Whoa! If the rich aren't getting into heaven, no one is!" But Jesus was saying, "God isn't looking for *upstanding people.* He's looking for people who will kneel down—he's looking for *kneeling-down people.*" The apostle Paul put it this way:

> When I came to you, brothers, I did not come with eloquence or superior wisdom as I proclaimed to you the testimony about God. For I resolved to know nothing while I was with you except Jesus Christ and him crucified. I came to you in weakness and fear, and with much trembling. My message and my preaching were not with wise and persuasive words, but with a

demonstration of the Spirit's power, so that your faith might not rest on men's wisdom, but on God's power. (1 Corinthians 2:1–5)

Paul didn't claim to be an upstanding person; he was a kneeling-down person. The load he carried was full of valuables, including a good family name, an outstanding education, and a flawless record of legalistic righteousness. But that heavy load came crashing down when Jesus confronted him on the road to Damascus. Paul let go of everything that made him powerful in human eyes; he laid down his self-sufficiency and picked up his cross to follow after Christ. As Paul later explained: "For to be sure, he was crucified in weakness, yet he lives by God's power. Likewise, we are weak in him, yet by God's power we will live with him to serve you" (2 Corinthians 13:4).

Arloa knows firsthand that God's power is manifested in weakness. She runs a food pantry on Chicago's East Side. She says God works miracles daily, but one incident stands out in her mind: "We operate a meal program and food pantry at our shelter. One day, we completely ran out of food after serving the evening meal. There was literally nothing left. We had no money, and the pantry was empty. There was nothing we could do from a human standpoint. But we could pray, so that's what we did. Then we went home that night, wondering what we would do the next day."

When they got to the shelter the following morning, they opened the doors to the food storage room, and it was completely full! Apparently, someone from Arloa's church worked at the post office. They had conducted a food drive and had so much extra food they decided to bring it to the shelter. Arloa says she has learned, "God supplies when we really have nothing left. We often don't experience God's power because we don't ever get to a place of truly needing God to provide."

Again, I challenge you to intentionally go where you cannot be self-sufficient. Kneel down—and watch God provide. When we are weak, we become vessels of the power of God.

Dear heavenly Father, forgive me for clinging to self-sufficiency. I've been struggling to understand why I don't see more of your power in my life. Now I understand. I've power-proofed my life. It's not what I set out to do, Lord Jesus. It comes out of my own fear and insecurity. I'm afraid if I don't take care of myself, no one else will. Teach me how to stop leaning on my own understanding but, instead, trust you entirely. Lord, I'm willing to be willing. I'm willing to lay aside everything that keeps me comfortable and to step out in faith. Well, at least I'm willing to try! Holy Spirit, I invite you to show me an opportunity to step out of my comfort zone within the next forty-eight hours. I'll be watching and praying for the right opportunity to come along. Help me to recognize it when it does. I want to experience your power! Amen.

AFFIRM

When I am weak, God is strong.

APPLY

1. Are you an upstanding person or a kneeling-down person? Explain your answer.

---

2. The Bible says when we humble ourselves, God will lift us up. Can you think of someone—a contemporary or biblical example—who humbled herself and God lifted her up? Describe.

---

3. The Bible also says God opposes the proud. Can you think of an example of a seemingly upstanding person who came crashing down? Again, cite a contemporary or biblical example.

---

4. Recall a time when you were weak—and God was strong.

---

5. Think of a situation for which your self-sufficiency would be inadequate for the task—something "out of your comfort zone." Describe. Would you be willing to go to that place to test and see if God will prove true to his Word: to be strong when you are weak?

_____

_____

_____

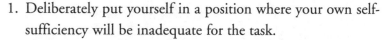

Act

1. Deliberately put yourself in a position where your own self-sufficiency will be inadequate for the task.
2. Write out today's affirmation and scripture in your index-card notebook.
3. Write out your own prayer, expressing what God has shown you today about his mighty power.

_____

_____

_____

_____

Watch for Open Doors of Opportunity

*Devote yourselves to prayer, being watchful and
thankful. And pray for us, too, that God may open
a door for our message, so that we may proclaim
the mystery of Christ, for which I am in chains.*

COLOSSIANS 4:2–3

We were back on the bus, ready to move on to our next ministry assignment. I was with a team of forty people as part of a Brio Missions trip to Peru, and we had just enjoyed an amazing response to our evangelistic outreach on a street corner in Lima. We stood amazed as the pandemonium of blaring horns, barking dogs, and jostling crowds faded into the background, enabling a large crowd of people to hear and respond to the gospel of Jesus Christ. Many prayed to receive Christ, and we took the time, in partnership with local Peruvian believers, to obtain their personal information for follow-up. Our work was done. Or so we thought.

Just before we pulled away, one of the teenagers, Emily Zerger, came rushing to the front of the bus. She said, "God is speaking to that man with the green backpack. I just know it. Look! Look at him sitting there! We need to send someone to talk to him." It was obvious to me that the Lord was speaking through Emily. Several men from our team approached the man, and he responded immediately. Soon, a group of American and Peruvian Christians gathered around this weeping man, who surrendered his life to God. As they prayed for him, the Lord spoke to one of our leaders, telling him that this man would be used in a mighty way to advance the kingdom of God in Peru.

Meanwhile, another Brio team was busy painting a local public school when one of the leaders, Dawn Youngblood, felt prompted to strike up a conversation with the principal. A friendship formed, and Dawn invited the principal to join her for lunch the next day, as it was our day off. The luncheon turned into a five-hour meeting that ended with this influential Peruvian surrendering her life to God and committing herself to his service and to the fulfillment of his purposes for her nation. Her husband and two sons are both active in the business and political life of the country, and Dawn believes God will use this family to reach the highest levels of their society.

Experiences like these are available to every devoted follower of Jesus Christ. God's power is not only for giving sight to the blind—although God's power can certainly do that and much more. The power of God is, first and foremost, for salvation. The power of God moves people from the kingdom of darkness into the kingdom of light.

The Christian life should be a daily adventure. We are not following a list of rules and regulations. We are following the Person of the Holy Spirit. He is always at work all around us. If we are not seeing his work, it's not because he isn't working! It's because we are not being prayerful and watchful.

I believe the greatest lesson the young people on our Brio Missions team learned was the inexpressible joy of being prayerful and watchful. What were they watching for? Evidence that God was working and inviting us to join him in that work. They discovered just how exciting it is to be a Christian when you pray and then expect God to show you where he's working. To become a vessel of God's power, we have to recognize the opportunities…and seize them.

Praying and watching isn't new, of course. It's what Nehemiah did thousands of years ago. Nehemiah served as cupbearer to the Babylonian king Artaxerxes during a time when the city of Jerusalem lay in ruins. When Nehemiah learned the extent of the damage, he fasted and prayed for God to give him an opportunity to speak with the king about the situation. "Lord, let your ear be attentive to the prayer of this your servant and to the prayer of your servants who delight in revering your name. Give your servant success today by granting him favor in the presence of this man" (Nehemiah 1:11). Then Nehemiah waited and watched for the right timing. He didn't bring up the subject, but instead waited until the king asked what was bothering him.

God had given Nehemiah an impossible assignment, requiring not only approval but massive provision from a pagan king. But when God opens a door of opportunity, nothing is impossible. The king provided Nehemiah with an armed entourage and the equivalent of millions of dollars in supplies. As a result, Nehemiah got the wall rebuilt within fifty-two days.

God has chosen us to advance his agenda for planet Earth. Sometimes that means we have to step out in faith to do things that, apart from God's power at work on our behalf, would end in disaster. This was true for Nehemiah, and it was true for Esther.

When Esther agreed to try to save her people, she prayed for God to grant her an opportunity to talk to a king—this time, the king was her own husband. But again, she didn't presume that, because of her position, she could rush in and make things happen. Instead, she prayed, then watched for the right opportunity, which didn't occur until she hosted a second banquet in her husband's honor. How did she know when the moment was right? I think it's safe to assume it was because she was being watchful and prayerful.

The scriptural examples just mentioned give us insight into how we can learn to recognize opportunities for becoming vessels of God's power. We are to *devote ourselves to prayer,* asking God to grant us the privilege of experiencing his power at work in the world. Then we are to *begin watching* for his answer to our prayer. But we *don't complain* when we don't see immediate results. Instead, we stay thankful. *God, I know you are working in the world. I am confident that today I'm going to experience your power. I'm on the watch!* As we maintain a thankful attitude, God provides an open door for us to proclaim his truth to someone. Some days, the open door will be offering someone a word of encouragement or giving someone a specific scripture, as God directs. Other days it will be to lead someone to Christ. But one thing is sure: when we pray, asking God for an open door to proclaim his truth, he will not fail to answer that prayer.

Dear heavenly Father, thank you that you are always at work in the world. Thank you that the Christian life is unlike any religion conceived by people. I am not following a list of rules and regulations; I have the joy of following the Person of the Holy Spirit. I want to know him better, to learn to recognize his voice and his work so I can get on board. Teach me to be watchful, alert to open doors to proclaim your truth. Heavenly Father, I thank you that you will open a door for me today…and I hereby commit myself to remain prayerful, watchful, and thankful until you do! Amen.

AFFIRM

God will open doors of opportunity for me.

APPLY

1. Are you devoted to prayer? What would this look like for you?

   _____

   _____

   _____

2. Recall a time when you were prayerful and watchful and, as a result, experienced the power of God.

   _____

   _____

   _____

3. Are you watchful as a matter of habit? How can you become more so?

_____

_____

_____

4. Think of a place you are likely to be in today (for example, a grocery store or the school parking lot). Pray specifically for God to show you his work in that place today.

_____

_____

_____

5. How would your life be different if you were devoted to prayer, watchful and thankful?

_____

_____

_____

*A*CT

1. Pray, then watch for open doors of opportunity to share the gospel or be of service to God.
2. Write out today's affirmation and scripture in your index-card notebook.

3. Write out your own prayer, expressing what God has shown you today about his mighty power.

_____

_____

_____

_____

Assert Your Spiritual Authority

I will give you the keys of the kingdom of heaven;
whatever you bind on earth will be bound in heaven,
and whatever you loose on earth will be loosed in heaven.

MATTHEW 16:19

On Day 18 you read about Mark and how God prompted him to pray concerning the statue of Artemis. Mark was praying in agreement with what God had revealed to be his will. That's why Mark didn't pray, *Dear God, if it's your will, please remove this statue.* Instead, when he prayed, he spoke directly to the statue. He wasn't wishy-washy about it either. He spoke with authority, *commanding* the statue to get in alignment with God's will. He commanded it to change form, a form that would represent the love and compassion of Jesus Christ.

Perhaps that strikes you as unusual.

Why would Mark speak to the statue, rather than speak to God about the statue? That's the question we'll explore today. There are different types of prayer. Some prayer is listening to the Father; some is speaking to the Father; but there is an oft-neglected form of prayer that Dr. Charles Kraft, professor at Fuller Theological Seminary and author of *I*

Give You Authority, calls "authority praying."[25] You do not need to abandon all other forms of prayer, but if you desire to experience more of
God's power, I encourage to explore praying with authority. In fact, when
you're done reading this book, read *I Give You Authority.* It will dramatically alter your perception about the level of power God intends for us to
experience.

In authority praying, you speak directly to the situation, as Jesus
instructed in Matthew 21:21: "I tell you the truth, if you have faith and
do not doubt, not only can you do what was done to the fig tree, but also
you can say to this mountain, 'Go, throw yourself into the sea,' and it will
be done." Notice Jesus did not say, "Pray to your Father in heaven and ask
him to remove the mountain." No. He said, "Tell the mountain to get out
of your way."

Many of us ask the Father to do things on our behalf in Jesus's
name. That's certainly a valid approach to prayer. But I just paged
through the book of Matthew, noticing how Jesus prayed. Remember,
in every one of these situations, Jesus was mentoring the disciples, showing them how they should conduct kingdom affairs. Here are some
examples I found:

Jesus spoke to a man's body, telling it to "be clean!" of leprosy (Luke
5:13). He didn't pray, *Dear heavenly Father, I pray that if it's your will, please
heal this man of leprosy.*

He healed the centurion's servant with a sentence directed toward her
boss: "Go! It will be done just as you believed it would" (Matthew 8:13).

Jesus delivered a demon-possessed man by speaking directly to the
demons, commanding them (not pleading with them) to "Go!" They
immediately submitted to his authority (see Matthew 8:28–32)—the
same authority he has delegated to us.

He healed a paralytic by speaking directly to the man, "Get up, take
your mat and go home" (Matthew 9:6). Again, notice he didn't bow his

head and pray, *Dear Father, please heal this man.* Jesus even states that his purpose in this situation was to demonstrate authority: "So that you may know that the Son of Man has authority on earth to forgive sins" (Matthew 9:6).

He healed two blind men by touching them, saying, "'According to your faith will it be done to you'; and their sight was restored" (Matthew 9:29–30).

When he healed a man with a shriveled hand, he commanded the man, "Stretch out your hand" (Matthew 12:13).

You may be thinking, *Okay, but Jesus didn't speak to statues.* Well, he spoke to winds and waves:

> Then [Jesus] got into the boat and his disciples followed him. Without warning, a furious storm came up on the lake, so that the waves swept over the boat. But Jesus was sleeping. The disciples went and woke him, saying, "Lord, save us! We're going to drown!"
>
> He replied, "You of little faith, why are you so afraid?"
>
> Then he got up and rebuked the winds and the waves, and it was completely calm. (Matthew 8:23–26)

Before Jesus rebuked the storm, he rebuked the disciples. Why? Because they had been imitating him long enough to have calmed the storm themselves. However, they were unable to do so because they panicked, and fear and faith are mutually exclusive. Jesus was asleep in the boat, because the storm didn't faze him in the least. From that centered place of calm, he was able to speak authoritatively *to the winds and waves,* "Be still!" (Mark 4:39).

On other occasions the Bible tells us people were amazed because Jesus taught as one with authority. He wasn't wishy-washy. We often respond to situations that grieve God's heart as if we don't know him at all. Do we really need to know if God wants to heal the sick? Are we really uncertain about God's view of oppressive situations? Didn't Jesus make it obvious when he walked the earth? He healed all who came to him in faith. He delivered all who were held captive but truly desired freedom.

I can think of one significant circumstance for which Jesus instructed us to speak *to God:* "Ask the Lord of the harvest, therefore, to send out workers into his harvest field" (Matthew 9:38). In other words, we are to ask God to send workers, but the workers must do the work of the kingdom. And how is kingdom work accomplished? By exercising our inherited rightful authority.

When Jesus sent out the first group of kingdom workers, "He called his twelve disciples to him and *gave them authority* to drive out evil spirits and to heal every disease and sickness" (Matthew 10:1, emphasis added). He further clarified, "As you go, preach this message: 'The kingdom of heaven is near.' Heal the sick, raise the dead, cleanse those who have leprosy, drive out demons" (Matthew 10:7–8).

Jesus told believers to exercise spiritual authority over the Enemy. He said, "I have been given all authority in heaven and on earth" (Matthew 28:18, NLT), then added, "I have given you [the disciples, which includes us] authority…to overcome all the power of the enemy" (Luke 10:19). If Jesus has *all* authority and has delegated that authority to us and given us the power "to overcome *all the power* of the enemy"—not just some of his power—we're foolish not to use that authority. Spiritual authority unleashes the power of God.

But in order to exercise spiritual authority, we must be in the right place, at the right time, doing the right thing. When we are not walking in obedience, God won't authorize us to do *anything for him.* Why would he? Consider a soldier who is not where he is supposed to be because he has gone AWOL. Imagine how effective this soldier would be if his commander left orders on his desk and the soldier returned six months later and tried to carry out those orders. It would be a disaster. The same is true in the spiritual realm. If we are not walking in obedience, God won't direct us to do anything for him. We can't exercise authority; all we can do is take matters into our own hands, behaving presumptuously. (Note: that's why it's vital to "wash and be cleansed" before stepping out in *any* ministry.)

Faith is a continuum, with unbelief at one extreme and presumption on the other. In other words, some Christians never expect God to answer *any* of their prayers. Others act as if God is their vending machine in heaven. Either extreme plays right into the devil's hand. Yet, frankly, I think God is far more pleased when we err on the side of presumption. His unrelenting rebuke of the Israelites for the sin of unbelief bears this out (see Hebrews 3:19). Of course, we don't want to be presumptuous either. That's why we have to stay in a close, intimate relationship with God, listening intently for his voice.

Let me give you an example of how you can exercise spiritual authority, thereby unleashing God's power. I often challenge women who were raised in godly homes to become Mighty Musk Ox Warrior Princesses.[26] The musk ox is a magnificent creature that lives in the Arctic region of the world, where wolves prey on it. The moment the adult musk oxen hear the dreaded howling of the wolves or even perceive danger nearby, they immediately form a protective circle around the weak and the young. The musk oxen will not run in the face of their enemies. Instead, the strong take their stand and lay down their lives to protect those who cannot protect themselves.

God gave me a powerful opportunity to see some Mighty Musk Ox Warrior Princesses exercise their spiritual authority at a recent event in Nebraska. On the last day of the retreat, a woman confided to me that her daughter had been among seven teenage girls who were held hostage at a Colorado high school. All of them were horribly abused during the three-hour ordeal and one was killed. When I asked this woman to tell her story to the group, 140 women formed a circle around her, proclaiming complete healing and restoration for her family through a supernatural work of God. Then we invited all the young women under age twenty-five to step into the circle. There was some initial hesitation, especially among the younger ones, but then as these mighty women proclaimed a shield of protection around their lives, the tears began flowing, and the tissues went flying.

Afterward, I talked with the young women, who all agreed it was among the most powerful spiritual experiences they had ever had—to listen as saints waged war on their behalf, taking authority over the forces of darkness in the name and by the blood of Jesus.

Of course, it's important not to get out of balance when it comes to exercising spiritual authority. The Bible warns us to be well balanced, because our adversary is prowling around "looking for someone to devour" (1 Peter 5:8)—and no doubt he will pounce on someone who is out of balance. Some Christians spend more time in prayer talking to the devil than they spend talking to God. That's ridiculous. *Most* of our time in prayer should be spent listening to God or praying his Word. Let's not waste hours bossing the devil around. Instead, let's brag about the cross— I suspect that topic of conversation sends demons running for cover anyway. If we're unsure whether a situation has demonic involvement, we can follow the pattern set forth by Dr. Kraft and proclaim, "If this is the work of the Enemy, I command you to stop it right now."

A final warning. I've known women who were "praying with authority" for their ex-husbands to return to them, as if they could make someone else bend to their will if they prayed long enough and hard enough. That's not faith; that's witchcraft. Witchcraft is trying to force our will on someone else. We might as well use a voodoo doll. If our objective is to control—whether God, people, or circumstances—then we are praying with wrong motives, and God will not honor such prayers.

We cannot use prayer to make God or people do what we want them to do, even if we want good things. I won't waste too much time beating the anti-name-it-and-claim-it drum, because I think enough writers are already doing that. Plus, I think God himself has addressed the weaknesses in that movement and brought some of its leading proponents back into balance. However, it's important to realize such theology, taken to its extreme, also comes dangerously close to witchcraft in its attempt to impose our will on God. Pretty scary.

Jesus delegated his authority to us for one reason and one reason only: so that we could pray for his kingdom to come and his will to be done on this earth, not so we could build our own mini-kingdoms or have our own will be done. As always, it's all about him.

⸺⸺◠

Dear heavenly Father, I thank you for the privilege you've granted me to exercise spiritual authority. Jesus, I acknowledge that all authority has been given to you. You delegated that authority to me for one purpose only: that I might pray for your kingdom to come and your will to be done on earth. Your will, not mine. Forgive me for those times when I've expected you to bend the knee to my wishes, rather than recognizing my position in service to you. I don't presume to understand all the implications of authority praying, but Holy Spirit, I am your student. Teach me your ways, and help me learn to walk in the full measure of spiritual authority that is rightfully mine. Amen.

AFFIRM

I can exercise my rightful spiritual authority.

APPLY

1. What do you think it means to exercise spiritual authority?

   _____

   _____

   _____

2. What are the potential pitfalls of misunderstanding spiritual authority?

   _____

   _____

   _____

3. What are the even greater potential pitfalls of failing to exercise our God-given spiritual authority?

_____

_____

_____

4. Describe a time when you or someone else exercised spiritual authority with dramatic results.

_____

_____

_____

5. What are some practical ways you can begin to exercise greater spiritual authority?

_____

_____

_____

$\mathcal{A}$CT

1. Pray the following prayer aloud over your household.

In the name of Jesus, I claim protection over my marriage, my children, and my household. I decree peace in our home and declare that the forces of darkness have no place here. We are devoted to God. No accusation can stand against this family, because God has granted us

*every spiritual blessing, and we are seated in heavenly places, hidden
with Christ in God. We stand arrayed in robes of righteousness,
dipped in the blood of the Lamb. Whatever forces might be planning
an attack to steal, kill, or destroy anything that belongs to this family,
I put you on notice that you are wasting your time. I command all
spiritual forces of wickedness under my rightful, blood-bought authority
to cease and desist. Holy Spirit, hem us in, behind and before. Be our
Wisdom, our Guide, our Strength, and our Protection. Thank you
that you live in me, and that you are far greater than he who lives in
the world. Jesus, we exalt your name and proclaim that your power
is greater than any other force. Thank you for the Cross. Amen.*

2. You might also want to bless your home with oil. You can purchase anointing oil from most Christian bookstores or ask your
   pastor if he can supply you with oil. If you prefer, you might ask
   a pastor, priest, or group of trusted prayer warriors to join you
   for this household blessing service.

3. To learn more about exercising spiritual authority, read *I Give
   You Authority* by Charles Kraft.

4. Write out today's affirmation and scripture in your index-card
   notebook.

5. Write out your own prayer, expressing what God has shown you
   today about his mighty power.

Be Faithful in Small Things

The King will say to those on his right, "Come, you who are blessed by my Father; take your inheritance, the kingdom prepared for you since the creation of the world. For I was hungry and you gave me something to eat, I was thirsty and you gave me something to drink, I was a stranger and you invited me in, I needed clothes and you clothed me, I was sick and you looked after me, I was in prison and you came to visit me."

Then the righteous will answer him, "Lord, when did we see you hungry and feed you, or thirsty and give you something to drink? When did we see you a stranger and invite you in, or needing clothes and clothe you? When did we see you sick or in prison and go to visit you?"

The King will reply, "I tell you the truth, whatever you did for one of the least of these brothers of mine, you did for me."

MATTHEW 25:34–40

*P*erhaps you read the last two chapters and thought, *I'm just not a bold person. I'd never have the nerve to walk up to a total stranger to tell him about Jesus.* If so, today is your day to receive special encouragement. That's because God's power is often seen when we are willing to do small things with great faithfulness. As Mother Teresa said, "We cannot all do great things, but we can do small things with great love."²⁷

For example, my husband, Jeff, has a standing appointment with a stranger. It's a different stranger every time, but as far as Jeff is concerned, it's a fixed appointment. Most Saturdays, he makes his weekly rounds of "hunting and gathering," as he likes to call it. Saturdays are his day to work on household projects, which invariably means buying this or that missing part. One of the stores on his regular route has a small concession stand located near the doorway. Every time Jeff shops there, he buys a soda on the way out to give away. He doesn't know who he'll give the soda to, but there's always someone thirsty in the desert. So Jeff buys the soda and then watches for someone to give it to.

Every follower of Jesus Christ has a standing appointment with people in need. If you see someone with a need that you can meet, consider it a divine appointment. You don't need to hear a chorus of angels singing to take the hint. If someone is thirsty, give that person something to drink. Hungry? Give them food. It's not that complicated. Don't overlook small opportunities just because they are small. Sometimes the power of God is most clearly demonstrated not in the big things, but in the small things we do with faithfulness.

Carol has an excellent policy. If she sees a homeless person and has even ten spare minutes, she drives through the nearest fast-food restaurant and buys that person food. It may not be a full-course meal, but she'll at least pick up a bag of French fries. Another friend keeps individually packaged snacks in her car (you know, the kind we put in our children's lunch bags). In her city, homeless people frequently stand by traffic lights. She rolls her window down to hand them a snack pack. No fanfare. No grandiose outreach program that requires months of planning. Just a quick demonstration of giving to Jesus by giving to others.

Sometimes we deceive ourselves into thinking outreach has to be splashy to be effective. We think we have to organize dozens of volunteers to march triumphantly into the inner city. Planned programs are fine, as long as we're not so busy planning them that we miss the person in need sitting right in front of us. It's not an either/or situation. We can and should do both.

When I lived in a small mountain community where 70 percent of the population received some form of government assistance, at least once a month I would go through my house, room by room, drawer by drawer, and gather up anything I didn't need, whether it was extra pots and pans, clothes I hadn't worn recently, or items that had been sitting in my pantry for a while. I'd call one of two women to help me load everything into a station wagon or minivan (depending upon which friend I called). If I was heading out of town on ministry, I would even empty out the refrigerator. My girlfriends would then give the items to people in need; the recipients never knew I was the giver, and I rarely discovered who the recipients were. It didn't matter. They had a need; we had more than we needed.

When an apartment building filled with Mexican immigrants burned to the ground, our family didn't need a special word from God to know what to do. My children and I tore through the house, searching for anything that might be a special blessing to these devastated people. They'd had precious little to start with; now they had nothing. They didn't even have insurance to replace their belongings. I was moved to tears when I saw how sacrificially my then-eight-year-old daughter, Tara, gave. She didn't restrict herself to items she no longer used, but gave away toys and clothing she still treasured.

We were overjoyed as we completely filled the back of our pickup.

Lest you are sitting there thinking to yourself, *Oh, that Donna is such a self-sacrificing saint,* let me set the record straight. A few days after the fire, I discovered that we had accidentally given away my dry-cleaning bag filled with some of my best "stage clothes," including a brand-new $150 Ann Taylor skirt I had obtained using a gift certificate. I had left the bag in the truck, planning to take it to the cleaners on Monday. We're talking hundreds of dollars worth of fabulous outfits that *actually fit me*—and you have no idea how hard it is to find clothes that *actually fit* my seriously weird shape. I cannot even tell you how tempted I was to track down that dry-cleaning bag. No, I mean, really! I even thought of asking the people for my bag back. Isn't that just pathetic? The thought of another woman wearing a skirt I only wore once tormented me for months; in fact, it still bugs me just a little. So, no, I am not a saint! I'm as selfish as anyone else—okay, probably *more* selfish. But I really didn't want to hear Jesus say, *Whatever you took back from those Mexican immigrants, you took back from me.*

So they kept the bag, and I made the most of a small opportunity.

When we think about the book of Acts, we typically focus on all the dramatic, miraculous events. While those events are certainly significant demonstrations of God's power, we also read about the seemingly small things:

All the believers were one in heart and mind. No one claimed that any of his possessions was his own, but they shared everything they had.... There were no needy persons among them. For from time to time those who owned lands or houses sold them, brought the money from the sales and put it at the apostles' feet, and it was distributed to anyone as he had need. (Acts 4:32, 34–35)

You may have noticed that I omitted verse 33 in the previous passage. Here's what it says: "With great power the apostles continued to testify to the resurrection of the Lord Jesus, and much grace was upon them all." Could there be a connection? Our faith is proved in how we treat people, especially those who are in need. We unleash God's power in many ways, large and small, whenever we are faithful to God.

Dear heavenly Father, thank you that there are opportunities for divine appointments all around me, every day of the week. Please open my heart to a world in need. I want to see Jesus in the lives of hurting people. I want to be his hands, his feet. Forgive me for all those times I deceived myself into waiting for a special invitation to reach out. Now I understand that a person in need is all the invitation I need. Help me to keep those standing appointments in your name. Amen.

AFFIRM

I can make the most of seemingly small opportunities.

APPLY

1. If you have a standing appointment with people in need, describe.

   _____

   _____

   _____

2. What is your response to the quote from Mother Teresa: "We cannot all do great things, but we can do small things with great love"? Can you think of another example of someone whose life exemplifies this quote? Describe.

   _____

   _____

   _____

3. Think of a situation you routinely encounter that might represent a standing appointment for you. Describe.

   _____

   _____

   _____

4. What are some practical ways you can be prepared to meet the needs of people who cross your path?

   _____

   _____

   _____

5. Has someone ever done something seemingly small for you, but it made a significant impact on you? Describe.

_____

_____

_____

ACT

1. Go through your house, room by room, drawer by drawer, closet by closet—and give away everything you can possibly spare. Set a specific date and, if possible, get your whole family involved.
2. Write out today's affirmation and scripture in your index-card notebook.
3. Write out your own prayer, expressing what God has shown you today about his mighty power.

_____

_____

_____

_____

Balance Solitude and Service

*Because so many people were coming and going
that they did not even have a chance to eat,
[Jesus] said to them, "Come with me by yourselves
to a quiet place and get some rest."*

MARK 6:31

*E*veryone talks about the hectic pace of life in the twenty-first century, and that observation is certainly true. But it's also obvious that the disciples kept up a fairly hectic pace themselves. In Mark 6, Jesus sent the twelve disciples out on a ministry trip. "They went out and preached that people should repent. They drove out many demons and anointed many sick people with oil and healed them" (verses 12–13). They returned, no doubt excited, but also drained from the spiritual battles they had waged. Shortly after their return, John the Baptist was beheaded. What an emotional blow to these men who believed that standing with Jesus meant a bright future, not a gory death. The news sobered them.

Knowing this, Jesus invited them to come away and rest. Even God knows we all need a well-deserved break from time to time. But on their way to peace and quiet, the disciples encountered a massive crowd. When they suggested sending everyone away (hey, don't be too tough on them, it was *Jesus's* idea for them to get away from it all), Jesus instead instructed them to feed five thousand people. Does that sound like your idea of a nap?

The book of Mark doesn't reveal exactly when the disciples finally got a break, but we can be certain that when Jesus expressed his concern and acknowledged their need to "come away and rest," he arranged time for that to happen. I'm sure it wasn't easy. It's never easy to get away and rest. It wasn't then. It isn't now. But it's vital for our long-term effectiveness that we balance solitude and service.

In recent years, I've become increasingly aware of my need to balance Christ's seemingly contradictory commands:

Come to me, all you who are weary and burdened, and I will give you rest. (Matthew 11:28)

Go into all the world and preach the good news to all creation. (Mark 16:15)

Sometimes I've wanted to say, "Jesus, make up your mind! Which one is it? Come or go?" I've had seasons in my life where I've done too much going—trying to save the world and driving myself half-crazy in the process. I would become so consumed with outreach that I neglected my health, my family, and even my spirit. Then I've swung to the other extreme, resting to the point of spiritual selfishness, where Christianity became all about me and my private journey with God.

Many devoted followers of Christ struggle to find that balance as well.

God has always commanded us to both come and go. There have always been those who willingly come, who sit at his feet and learn, and learn, and learn. But they never get up out of the pew to go. Then there are others who gladly go, but who sometimes do more harm than good because they do not first seek God, are not securely grounded in him, and don't return to him before they are depleted. God calls us to experience a divine rhythm:

- Come to God to get our needs met, go to meet the needs of others.
- Come to learn, go to teach.
- Come to be filled, go to pour forth.
- Come to be ministered to, go to minister.

Just as there is a need for both spiritual fruit and spiritual gifts, there's a need for both inward spiritual reality and practical outreach. Again, some churches emphasize outreach and feature countless social programs. Unfortunately, they fail to emphasize the importance of the deeper spiritual life and consider prayer, fasting, and meditation as unproductive. Other churches offer intense spiritual programs, but their members rarely leave the building. There's even a divide within many churches—the outreach department fighting for bulletin space with the spiritual-enrichment department, each sincerely convinced that the other has the wrong set of priorities.

We need both. We need balance, and we need each other to help us *stay* balanced. But practically speaking, how is that accomplished? Dietrich Bonhoeffer said the church would experience revival through the emergence of what he called a new monasticism. By that he meant the blending of a quiet, contemplative, devotional life with an outreach-minded, service-oriented faith that's an active, contagious demonstration of God's power.

If the idea of becoming a monk doesn't appeal to you, it's probably because you're unfamiliar with the new monasticism. Its focus is not so much on celibacy—although that movement is gaining momentum, particularly among young people in Europe—but upon community. The basic premise is that the power of God—the power to transform us inwardly and the power to transform society as we reach outward—requires a radical commitment. Commitment is most effectively carried out within the context of a close-knit Christian community that balances the need for inward spiritual reality with outward, practical ministry.

While traveling in Turkey in 2005, I met a remarkable Anglican priest who is taking the call to a new monasticism seriously. John Skinner and his wife, Linda,[28] are best known as cofounders of an innovative monastic community in Northumbria, England. The Northumbria Community takes its inspiration from Lindisfarne, often called Holy Island. At times, water surrounds Lindisfarne, but at other times it's a peninsula. More than a thousand years ago, Celtic monks began inhabiting this beautiful island-peninsula. During the island times of isolation, they focused on seeking God wholeheartedly through study and meditation, while deepening their relationships with one another. But then, when the land bridge formed, the monks crossed over to the world beyond, sharing the gospel, ministering practically to the needs of the people, and demonstrating the miraculous power of God through healing and head-to-head battles with Druid priests and pagan gods.

Celtic monks weren't self-centered isolationists. They weren't communing with God for the sake of communing with God. They were finding rest for their souls *in preparation* for taking the gospel into all the world. They were both missions minded and outreach oriented. As a result of discovering the beautiful balance of resting and serving, coming and going, inward spiritual reality and practical outreach, Celtic monks were among the most effective evangelists in church history. They not only treasured and preserved the Scripture and early church history, they took the gospel all over Europe. On foot and in tiny, makeshift boats, they ultimately traveled as far east as Russia and as far west as Greenland and Iceland; and there's even compelling evidence that they made it to North America. They fulfilled Christ's command to make disciples, with signs and wonders following.

Celtic monks were powerfully effective in fulfilling the Great Commission, precisely because they discovered what they called "the ebb and flow" or the divine rhythm. The rhythm of rest and service. The rhythm of coming and going. Sometimes we must be surrounded by the Living Water; we must allow the Spirit of God to wash over us, healing and restoring our lives as we quietly rest in his presence. It's the only cure for spiritual dehydration! Other times we must go forth, taking the Living Water to a parched world.

Many Christians today lack this rhythm. I believe this is another reason why we are not experiencing the power of God to the degree that God desires. We need to rediscover the ebb and flow; we need to discover the divine rhythm.

~~⌐

Dear heavenly Father, I need your wisdom and grace to live in accordance with divine rhythm. I want to walk in obedience and in a balanced way, carrying out your commands to come and to go. Holy Spirit, help me to heed your voice. I trust you to tell me when it's time to sit and learn; when it's time to be surrounded by the Living Water. But also, to discern when it's time to go forth in ministry. Teach me the divine rhythm of life. Amen.

AFFIRM

I experience God's power when I walk in divine rhythm.

APPLY

1. What does divine rhythm mean to you?

_____

_____

_____

2. Are you more willing to come to Jesus...or go to all the world?

_____

_____

_____

3. How can you balance your natural tendency toward either coming or going?

_____

_____

_____

4. Describe what the divine rhythm might look like for your life. What are some practical ways you can incorporate balanced coming and going?

_____

_____

_____

5. Why do you think it's important to have a community of believers who support your desire to balance coming and going? How can you cultivate such a community?

_____

_____

_____

ACT

1. Talk with others about the concept of a new monasticism. Discuss who in your circle of influence is strong in their natural desire to come to Jesus and who is more eager to go at his command. How can you support and benefit from one another?

2. Write out today's affirmation and scripture in your index-card notebook.

3. Write out your own prayer, expressing what God has shown you today about his mighty power.

_____

_____

_____

_____

Keep Believing

I have fought the good fight, I have
finished the race, I have kept the faith.

2 TIMOTHY 4:7

I have experienced the power of God around the world in every setting imaginable. But you don't have to be a world traveler to see
God's power at work. Yesterday I took a break from writing to eat lunch,
and the thought occurred to me: *Why not tap into the iTunes library on my*
laptop to listen to some worship music? So I selected a song featuring the
refrain: "You are good, you are good, and your love endures."

I started thinking about God's enduring love in my own life, and I
was driven to my knees.

My father passed away on June 19, 2006. I was with him when he
died, which is a miracle since we lived three thousand miles apart. But
God, in his infinite mercy, arranged for me to be present for my father's
homegoing. I believe God sent me to help my dad make the trip. It had
been almost one year since we had prayed together and Dad acknowledged his need for a Savior. As he wrestled to let go of his life, what clearly

brought him the most peace was when I prayed aloud or read God's Word to him. Dad died peacefully, and the room was filled with peace for thirty minutes after he left. As I sat quietly, I knew I was experiencing the power of God.

I had been a Christian for twenty-six years, and if anyone during any of those years had told me that one day I would sit at my father's death-bed enveloped in peace, I wouldn't have believed it. Throughout my youth, Dad and I had a very stormy relationship. Trust me: Irish dad plus rebellious Irish daughter is a volatile combination. Although we experienced a beautiful restoration during my freshman year of college, the one subject we could never discuss was my faith. It was off-limits. I think he secretly suspected I had joined a cult or, at the very least, was a religious fanatic.

But in the end, we understood each other. Faith was our common bond as he looked into my eyes and breathed his last. The only way the presence of God could have been more real would've been for Jesus himself to walk into the room. I knew that I knew my father was on his way to heaven; more important, I think my father finally knew it too. Of all the gifts God has given me, I believe that moment is one of the greatest.

As I sat there eating my lunch and thinking about the miracle of my dad's homegoing, I suddenly recalled scene after scene of God's powerful intervention in my life. I thought about where I was when God reached down to rescue me, the amazing places he's taken me, the incredible opportunities I've been given.

As all these thoughts flashed through my mind, I could no longer contain my joy. Without even thinking about what I was doing, I jumped up and started dancing around the empty retreat center cafeteria. I was overwhelmed with the awareness of how powerful God is.

Just then, one of the staff workers walked in.

People must just wonder about me. But that's okay. I was caught up in the wonder of God, and I make no apologies for that.

On Day 1, I challenged you to give God thirty days—and see what he would do. Let me issue an even greater challenge: give God the rest of your life—and see what he will do. I promise you, he's just getting started! So keep believing. God really does want you to become a vessel of his power.

⸻

Dear heavenly Father, thank you that the power of God isn't just something that Christians experience in faraway countries. I'm glad that I don't have to leave the country to experience it myself. I thank you that your power is available right here, right now, in my own life, within my own family. And maybe, just maybe, that's the greatest miracle of all. Holy Spirit, I invite you to work through me to touch the lives of my family and friends. I believe you can and will show me your power at work in the lives of those closest to me. Amen.

Affirm

I choose to keep believing.

APPLY

1. Is there a person in your life you've tried to (or at least wanted to) share your faith with for many years? Is it hard for you to keep believing God can touch that person's life through you? Why or why not?

   _____

   _____

   _____

2. Describe a time when you experienced the power of God at work in someone close to you.

   _____

   _____

   _____

3. Thirty days ago, you decided to "give God thirty days—and see what he will do." Reflect on the last thirty days. What are some things you've seen God do in your life?

   _____

   _____

   _____

4. How has your understanding of God—and your role as a vessel of his power—changed over the last thirty days? Write out an example.

----

5. In what area do you need to keep believing that God will show his power? Write it below and then commit to pray daily concerning it.

----

*A*CT

1. Take time to review—and possibly expand—your answers to the previous questions 3 and 5. Share these thoughts with one or two friends who can celebrate with you and commit to join you in praying for those areas where you need to keep believing.
2. Put on some praise music and worship God with all your might, even if that means getting up and dancing!
3. Write out today's affirmation and scripture in your index-card notebook.
4. Write out your own prayer, expressing what God has shown you over the past thirty days about his mighty power.

Becoming a
Vessel of God's Power

1. I can experience the power of God.
2. I remain confident that God is still a God of power.
3. I choose to remember the works of God.
4. If I want to experience God's power, I must align myself with his purposes.
5. The power of God flows most consistently through pure vessels.
6. Confession and cleansing set me free to serve God.
7. The power of God will keep flowing as long as I am purified daily.
8. I choose a lifestyle of radical purity.
9. I need a PIT crew: prayer warriors, insightful counselors, and gifted teachers.
10. There's no substitute for time spent in God's Word.
11. When I customize my Bible, I am sharpening my sword.
12. God's Word has the power to transform me, especially when I make it personal.
13. God's power is unleashed through me as I share his Word with others.
14. I am an imitator of God.
15. God has called me to exercise bold faith.
16. I believe God likes to say yes to my prayers.
17. Praying God's Word unleashes God's power in my life.
18. I believe there's power in God-prompted prayer.

19. There's power in prayer when two or three are gathered.
20. I can find rest for my soul.
21. I acknowledge my faith in God's power by choosing to take a day off each week.
22. I believe God keeps his promises.
23. I can behave as God's child.
24. The Holy Spirit gives me power within and power upon my life.
25. When I am weak, God is strong.
26. God will open doors of opportunity for me.
27. I can exercise my rightful spiritual authority.
28. I can make the most of seemingly small opportunities.
29. I experience God's power when I walk in divine rhythm.
30. I choose to keep believing.

PERSONALIZED SCRIPTURES

Please see Day 12 for insight on the importance
of making God's Word personal.

I am one of God's treasured possessions. He handpicked me to be his own. (Deuteronomy 26:16–19)

I can either magnify God or magnify my problems. I choose to magnify God. (Psalm 69:30–31)

My family is blessed when we come in and blessed when we go out. (Deuteronomy 28:6)

I meditate on God's Word day and night. I love to memorize Scripture! (Psalm 119:97)

I know that life and death are in the power of the tongue. So I let the words of my mouth and the meditations of my heart be acceptable before God. (Psalm 19:14)

I enjoy life and peace because I keep my mind fixed on the things of God. When my life lacks peace, I refocus my mind on him and my peace is restored. (Isaiah 26:3)

God shows me the way to go. (Proverbs 3:5–8)

My soul is satisfied with the things of God. (Psalm 84:1–2)

I remember all God's benefits: He forgives me, heals me, and surrounds me with loving-kindness. He has rescued me from an eternity in hell and has blessed me in this life as well. (Psalm 103:1–5)

I don't waste my time looking for "the speck" in other people's eyes. Instead, I focus on removing the plank from my own eye—realizing "the plank" is my own critical spirit. (Matthew 7:3–5)

I trust in God, and he shows me the way I should go. (Psalm 143:8)

I spend time with people who are wise, so I will become wise. (Proverbs 13:20)

I am fearfully and wonderfully made. (Psalm 139:13–16)

I know nothing is impossible with God. (Luke 1:37)

The Enemy may come against me one way, but he'll be forced to flee from me seven ways! (Deuteronomy 28:7)

I trust in the Lord with all my heart rather than trying to figure things out for myself. (Proverbs 3:5–8)

I lay up for myself treasures in heaven. I do not store treasure here on earth. I realize that where my treasure is, there my heart will also be. (Matthew 6:19–21)

I have absolutely no regrets because all things work together for my good, because I love God and have been called according to his purpose. (Romans 8:28)

The more I fill my mind with whatever is true, noble, excellent and praiseworthy, the less room there is in my mind for negative thoughts. Therefore, I choose to think about such things. (Philippians 4:8–9)

I love giving, because I know that in the same measure I give, it will be given back to me—good measure, pressed down, shaken together, and running over. (Luke 6:38)

I guard my mouth and keep myself from trouble. (Proverbs 21:23)

I am more than a conqueror through Christ who loved me. (Romans 8:37)

I am not easily provoked. (1 Corinthians 13:5)

I enjoy every spiritual blessing! (Ephesians 1:3)

I diligently guard my heart, because I know out of it flow the issues of life. (Proverbs 4:23)

When I call to God, he answers me. He tells me things I wouldn't know otherwise. (Jeremiah 33:3)

No weapon that's formed against me will prosper. All those who rise up against me will fall. Every accusation made against me will be refuted. (Isaiah 54:17)

I am confident that God will reward me as I diligently seek him. I don't know what form the reward will take, but I know it will be awesome. (Hebrews 11:6)

I know today will be a great day, because God's mercies are new every morning. (Lamentations 3:23)

I've made it my goal to be steadfast, unmovable, always abounding in the work of the Lord. (1 Corinthians 15:58)

I am persuaded that nothing can separate me from the love of God. (Romans 8:38–39)

I let the peace of Christ rule in my heart. (Colossians 3:15–16)

I am a slave to righteousness. I am no longer free to live however I please. (Romans 6:19–23)

I know God is able to do exceedingly abundantly above all that I could possibly ask or imagine. (Ephesians 3:20)

Today I will know firsthand the love of Christ, which passes knowledge, and I will be filled with the fullness of God. (Ephesians 3:19)

Any hardships I face in this world are nothing compared to the glory that will be revealed in me. (Romans 8:18)

God will bring something good out of every circumstance, even if I don't understand the how, when, or why. (Romans 8:28)

I'm not going to be afraid of anything today, because God has not given me a spirit of fear but of love, power, and a sound mind. (2 Timothy 1:7)

I am a jar of clay, but I contain a heavenly treasure. God's power is at work in me. (2 Corinthians 4:7)

The One who began a good work in me will see it through to completion. (Philippians 1:6)

I reap what I sow. Therefore, I choose to sow wisely. (Galatians 6:7–9)

I always choose to offer the sacrifice of praise and thanksgiving. (Hebrews 13:15)

Greater is he who is in me than he who is in the world. (1 John 4:4)

I firmly believe God desires for me to prosper and enjoy good health. (3 John 2)

God gives me power and increases my strength. I run and am not weary. I walk and do not faint. (Isaiah 40:28–31)

My vindication comes from God, so I don't waste time trying to prove I'm right. (Isaiah 54:17)

NOTES

1. Thanks to the men of River of Life Church, Phoenix, Arizona, for sharing their inspirational testimonies with me.
2. As a former gymnast and runner, I know all about pulled muscles, and I assure you, they do not heal in two hours!
3. For more information, please visit www.celebraterecovery.com.
4. If you are often tripped up by offenses, I recommend that you read *Bait of Satan* by John Bevere.
5. Gregory Frizzell, *Returning to Holiness: A Personal and Churchwide Journey to Revival* (Memphis: Master Design, 2000), ix–x.
6. In his book *Returning to Holiness,* Dr. Frizzell explores each of these areas in great detail: sins of thought, attitude, speech, relationships, commission, and omission. It is an excellent resource for individuals and churches seeking revival. I highly recommend it.
7. For more information, visit http://en.wikipedia.org/wiki/Act_of_Contrition.
8. For more information on Tina Marie's ministry, visit www.tina marielive.com.
9. In this particular country, women wear either modest clothing and beautiful head scarves or traditional covering, but not to the extreme seen in countries under the Taliban. Their faces were almost always showing, but they believed in covering their hair. Many of the women looked spectacular—modest, but very chic.
10. Check out www.bsfinternational.org for a class near you.
11. This account is shared in a Brio Missions promotional brochure. Visit www.briomag.com/missions for more details.

12. For more information, please see "William Carey's Amazing Mission," Christian History Institute, *Glimpses,* http://chi.gospelcom .net/GLIMPSEF/Glimpses/glmps045.shtml.

13. For more information, please see "William Carey's Amazing Mission."

14. For more information, please see www.careyoutreach.org/Carey.htm and "William Carey's Amazing Mission."

15. For more information, please see www.hectortorres.org.

16. For more information, please see PrayerQuake. This is from a presentation by Dee Duke, 10 June 2004, Mesa, Arizona.

17. This story was told to me by a pastor's wife at a retreat in South Carolina. I regret that I do not recall the woman's name, but I believe this story is true.

18. This information was taken from Daniel Henderson, Praying with Power Conference, Central Christian Church, Mesa, Arizona, 4 November 2006.

19. Pastor Henderson was gracious enough to share this insight, including the Greek spelling, in a private conversation held during one of the breaks at the Praying with Power Conference.

20. "Listening to the Fathers," *CrossPoint,* Fall 2000 (Brewster, MA: Paraclete), 27.

21. You can order them through the Web site, www.pottersplace.net. Please consider supporting these dear friends by purchasing their beautiful handmade pottery.

22. These statistics were presented by Daniel Henderson at the Praying with Power Conference.

23. For more information, please see www.billygraham.org.

24. This information was taken from a message by Scot Anderson at Living Word Bible Church, Mesa, Arizona, 9 November 2006.

25. Charles Kraft, *I Give You Authority* (Grand Rapids: Chosen, 1997), 52.

26. Visit www.donnapartow.com/muskox if you'd like to read more about the history and mission of the Mighty Musk Ox Warrior Princess Brigade.

27. For more information, please see http://www.quotedb.com/quotes/1865.

28. The new monasticism incorporates married couples as well as entire families.

ACKNOWLEDGMENTS

Special thanks to…

- Susie Shellenberger, Kathy Gowler, and the team at Brio Missions. Most of all, thanks to my *amazing* teams: Team Uno and Cinqo de Feugo! You showed me what power-packed faith is all about. Many of the stories in this book were inspired by you. I love you so much.

- The staff of The Community of Living Water in Cornville, Arizona, for great hospitality and fabulous cooking.

- My PIT crew—thanks for praying, counseling, teaching, and stretching; but most of all, thanks for loving me, flaws and all.

- My online discussion group contributors: Vicki Bedford, Darsi Brinley, Betty P. Culley, Patty Dietz, Tammy Dowell, Crystal Dunlap, Kim Frisbee, Virginia Garrett, Barbara Graydon, Cindy Hannon, Jenni Hurst, Judy Lovitt, Doreen McPherson, Janice Miller, Susan Mynyk, Jodi Nagy, Marisol Rodriguez, Brenda Schmid, Margaret Scovell, Judy Sheridan, Lyn Souter, Claudia Weemes, Donna Woodfill.

About the Author

Donna Partow is a best-selling author and Christian communicator with a compelling testimony of God's transforming power. Her previous books, including *Let Your Life Count* and *Becoming a Vessel God Can Use,* have sold almost a million copies on all seven continents and have been translated into numerous languages, such as Arabic, Chinese, German, Portuguese, Indonesian, Korean, Mongolian, and Spanish.

Donna's unique message cuts across social, cultural, and denominational barriers. She ministers to the homeless, alcoholics, drug addicts, and battered women in various inner cities, but she is also a popular speaker at rural women's conferences and has a special love for islands. She's prayed with a Muslim convert in an underground cave in Turkey and with new believers in the jungles of Papua New Guinea. Donna has been privileged to speak at the CIA headquarters on two separate occasions, and she has also shared her faith on crowded street corners in South America.

To learn more about Donna's ministry, or if your church or organization would like to invite her to speak, visit www.donnapartow.com. Her Web site is filled with practical tools to help you transform your life so God can transform the world through you.

GOD WANTS TO USE YOU!

You may be the answer to someone's prayer!
Discover how God can use you, wherever you are,
when you walk with him daily.

To learn more about WaterBrook Press and view
our catalog of products, log on to our Web site:
www.waterbrookpress.com

WATERBROOK
PRESS